THE WORTH OF WATER

THE WORTH OF

WATER

Our Story of Chasing Solutions to the World's Greatest Challenge

Gary White *and* Matt Damon

Portfolio / Penguin

Portfolio / Penguin
An imprint of Penguin Random House LLC
penguinrandomhouse.com

Most Portfolio books are available at a discount when purchased in quantity for
sales promotions or corporate use. Special editions, which include personalized covers,
excerpts, and corporate imprints, can be created when purchased in large quantities.
For more information, please call (212) 572-2232 or email specialmarkets@
penguinrandomhouse.com. Your local bookstore can also assist with discounted bulk
purchases using the Penguin Random House corporate Business-to-Business
program. For assistance in locating a participating retailer, email
B2B@penguinrandomhouse.com.

Insert image credits: photographs by Todd Williamson for Water.org, p. 1 (top), p. 6
(middle, bottom); photographs courtesy of Water.org, p. 1 (bottom), p. 2, p. 3 (bottom),
p. 5 (bottom), p. 6 (top), p. 7 (bottom), p. 8; photograph by J. Tayloe Emery courtesy of
DATA, p. 3 (top); photograph by Taylor Davidson courtesy of Clinton Global Initiative,
p. 4 (bottom); photograph by Paul Morse courtesy of Clinton Global Initiative, p. 4
(middle); photograph by Juliana Thomas courtesy of Clinton Global Initiative, p. 4
(top); photograph by Praveen Sundaram for Water.org, p. 5 (top); photograph by Jakob
Polacsek for World Economic Forum, p. 7 (middle); photograph by Simone D.
McCourtie for World Bank Group, p. 7 (top).

ISBN 9780593189979 (hardcover)
ISBN 9780593189986 (ebook)

Printed in the United States of America
1st Printing

BOOK DESIGN BY CHRIS WELCH

Some pseudonyms have been used to protect the privacy of the individuals involved.

This book is dedicated to the resilient,
resourceful, inspiring people we serve.
By investing in safe water and all the enormous
possibilities it brings, you are charting
a new course—not only for yourselves and
your families, but for all humanity.

When the well's dry, we know the worth of water.

—BENJAMIN FRANKLIN

Contents

THE WORTH OF WATER

1

WHAT THE HELL IS THE "WATER ISSUE"?

POV: Matt Damon

I've spent most of my life telling stories on-screen, not on the page—so as I was thinking about how to begin this book, I thought about how I'd start the movie. We'd fade in on a hut I visited in rural Zambia in 2006. I can still see it clearly in my mind: earthen brick walls, dirt floor, thatched roof. The landscape around it was usually dry, but because this was April, the end of the rainy season, the ground was covered, in parts, with a thin blanket of green. I was sitting outside the hut, waiting for a teenager to get home from school.

I was in Zambia because Bono—the rock star who spends his spare time fighting to end extreme poverty—had been pestering me to go. "Pest" is Bono's word. He wears it like a badge of honor. He takes pride in getting people—politicians especially, but others, too—to do things they wouldn't otherwise do, if he wasn't pestering them. The guy is really good at it. Bono believes that seeing poverty up close can change a person's priorities, can compel them to go out and do something about it. So he and his colleagues at the organization he started, DATA—which would eventually become the ONE Campaign—had been pressuring me to join them on a trip to Africa. He'd been pressuring me with the zeal of a telemarketer. He was not going to take no for an answer.

My answer wasn't no, exactly. I just had a lot going on in my life. My wife would be seven months pregnant at the time of the trip, and I had only a small window of time before my next movie. So I told Bono it just wasn't a good time. He looked at me and said, "It's *never* going to be a good time." Which, of course, was totally right.

I had no grand illusions about the point of going on this trip. It's not like I'd be changing anybody's life. Bono likes to say that there's nothing worse than a rock star with a cause, but an actor with a cause is a close second. I winced at the mental image of me walking through the bush or an urban slum somewhere, looking concerned, and then flying home to my comfortable life. But then I thought: that's an even dumber excuse for not going than "I'm busy." The more I thought about the trip, the more I realized that I wanted to go and meet some of the people who live in these extremely poor places, to see firsthand the challenges they face, and to figure out whether there was something I could be doing to help. So I told Bono I'd go, and my older brother, Kyle, agreed to come along, too.

The trip was about two weeks long. It took us to slums and rural villages across South Africa and Zambia. DATA had set it up like a college mini course. Each day, we learned about a different challenge that kept people from breaking the cycle of poverty: underfunded health systems, the challenges of life in a slum, the HIV/AIDS crisis. We read briefing books about each issue, visited organizations that were trying to tackle them, and, most important, talked with the people.

On one of our last days in Zambia, we were going to learn about water. It wasn't clear to me why. I understood why we had been focusing on HIV/AIDS and education—these were issues that you read about in the news, issues that people talked about or signed petitions about or donated in support of. But when I heard we'd be spending the day on the "water issue," I wasn't sure what issue that was, exactly. I guessed the water was contaminated.

Then I read my issue brief. It said, yes, the water was contaminated—so much so that waterborne diseases were killing a child about every twenty seconds.[1] But the water was also hard to access. There were no water pipes in these villages, no water taps in people's homes. Somebody had to go get the water and bring it back, and that somebody was almost always a woman or a girl. This was their responsibility: to walk as far as necessary to whatever water source they could find and fill their plastic jerrican, a five-gallon water jug that weighs more than forty pounds when full.[2] Then they turn around and carry it home. And the next day they wake up and do it again.

To see what that was like, we drove four hours from

Zambia's capital, Lusaka, to a village with a well that a part-ner of DATA's helped build. The staff knew of a family who lived close to the road. Their daughter Wema* was fourteen, and ev-ery day after school she walked to the well to get water for her family. She'd agreed to let us walk with her, but when we ar-rived at her home, it was empty. Not just the home, but the whole area. There was no village center that I could see; all the huts were spread out. It was very still, very quiet, and we just sat there for a while, waiting.

Eventually we saw Wema coming toward us down the path. She was carrying books and wearing a simple blue dress that looked like a school uniform. She greeted us shyly, then put down her books and went to fetch her family's jerrican.

At first, as we started walking to the well, the conversation was awkward. Which wasn't really a surprise. Wema, who wal-ked alone to this well every day, suddenly had an entourage of trip coordinators and village officials, plus an overeager movie actor. She and I didn't speak the same language, so we had to rely on an interpreter. Still, as we walked, everybody else hung back a bit, giving us some space. Her responses to my questions were pretty short, but after a while we both relaxed a little, and even the silences felt natural enough. It was a peaceful walk down a country road.

After half an hour or so, we arrived at the well. Somebody suggested I try my hand at it. I had just finished filming one of the Jason Bourne movies, so I thought I was in pretty good

---

* To protect her privacy, we've used a pseudonym.

shape. But pumping water from this well was harder than it looked. Wema and I laughed as I struggled with it. She had this incredibly practiced way of working the pump and then hefting this big, heavy yellow can up onto her head, where she kept it balanced with the help of one hand. This was easy to admire until you remembered (if you'd let yourself forget) that this was work for her: an inescapable, essential chore.

On our way back, it started to rain. Nobody said anything about it; we just kept walking. There's something about succumbing to the rain and accepting you're going to get soaked that loosens people up. The conversation got easier. I asked the girl if she wanted to live in the same village when she grew up. She smiled at me, a little shy again—as if she was debating whether or not to answer. After a moment, she did. "I want to go to Lusaka," she said, "and become a nurse."

I had this feeling that she mostly kept this ambition to herself. I wondered if her parents even knew, and if she'd hesitated to tell me because I might tell them. It was no small thing for her to have this dream—to think about leaving the place she'd always known, to head out on her own and show what she could do. It really resonated with me. And look, I know it's a cliché to meet someone halfway across the world whose life is dramatically different from your own, and suddenly see yourself in them—but I did. She brought to mind that feeling of restlessness, that eagerness to get out and do something new, somewhere new. I knew exactly what it felt like to be a teenager with a dream. I spent my teenage years pooling the money from my summer jobs in a joint bank account with Ben Affleck so we could move to New York and become actors. Not the same thing, obviously. But not so different that we couldn't connect.

As I talked with her, it seemed clear to me that she was going to do it. She had a spark, a kind of self-possession that made it easy for me to imagine that one day, she'd work up the courage to tell her parents she was going to chase her dream to Lusaka. Maybe they'd be angry about that, or sad about losing her, or proud that she was thinking big. Maybe all three. But she'd study, and she'd work, and she'd meet her goal. More than fifteen years later I'm still convinced she's made it. That she's not still walking that path and carrying that jerrican. I hope I'm right.

The main reason I'm optimistic—actually, the only reason I can be optimistic—is that Wema was able to go to school. It took half an hour to walk to the well we visited, but an hour of walking every day left her enough time to attend school and do her homework before the sun set—the village had no electricity, so after dark it was impossible to read a book. DATA introduced me to her because she was, in relative terms, a success story—a girl lucky enough to have a well close by so she could spend a good part of her days learning. Millions of girls aren't so lucky. For them, getting water doesn't take one hour; it takes three or four or six. It's what they do: they walk for water. That necessity keeps them from going to school, or working in the fields to earn money for their families, or creating something they can sell at a market. In fact, in some regions of India, water is so scarce that men take "water wives"—second and even third wives who spend all day, every day, gathering water for the family.[3]

I kept coming back to that old adage: "Water is life." How many hours of that fourteen-year-old's life had already been saved because someone thought to dig a well a mile away from her house instead of four or five? That decision was the reason she could spend her days doing more than walking to and from the well. It was the reason she was able to pursue a dream that felt so big and audacious she hesitated even to say it out loud. For Wema, water was life; it was also a shot at a better life.

I should probably pause right here to acknowledge that the "celebrity goes to Africa and resolves to change the world" thing has probably triggered your gag reflex. It triggers mine, too. I might, in fact, be that celebrity, but I am also my mother's son.

My mom, Nancy Carlsson-Paige, who's in her seventies now, was a professor of early childhood education when I was growing up. She taught at Lesley University in Cambridge, Massachusetts. From the time I was nine years old, I lived with my mom and brother in a six-family communal house near the school. You know when people complain about the liberal bias of academia, and they paint some ludicrous picture of a kind of super-bookish hippie commune? Yeah, I grew up there. No joke, one of my babysitters was Howard Zinn, the famous Boston University professor who wrote *A People's History of the United States* and helped lead the movement to teach history from the perspective of oppressed people rather than the people who did the oppressing. When people call me a Hollywood liberal, part of me wants to fight back—and part of me just wants to say, "Well, Cambridge, not Hollywood."

During my teenage years in the eighties, one of the big issues you heard a lot about in Cambridge (not at the places where Ben and I were hanging out in Central Square, but definitely around my dinner table) was the upheaval in Central America. The roots of the crisis went back to the 1950s, when the Eisenhower administration ordered the CIA to help overthrow the democratically elected president of Guatemala on the notion that it would stop the spread of communism in our hemisphere. Guatemala's president was just a left-wing social reformer, not a Communist, but the fear he might secretly be one, or might someday become one, was enough for the United States to support a military coup. Two hundred thousand people died in the civil war that followed.[4] In the seventies and eighties, leftist movements in the region—the Sandinistas in Nicaragua and the FMLN in El Salvador—overthrew a dictatorship and a military junta, respectively. The United States backed the dictators, giving them the training and funding to conduct long and bloody civil wars. There were terrible human rights violations on both sides, but there's too much tragic history to cover in this book—anyhow, I know some people aren't going to trust a guy who first learned history from Howard Zinn to tell it.

Suffice it to say that when I was growing up, Cambridge was a major center of resistance to these policies. You'd see churches hosting memorials for victims of political oppression; you'd run into community volunteers walking door to door carrying pictures of war victims, raising money for them. I remember big protests in Boston Common—including one where five hundred people occupied the JFK Federal Building. My mom went to these protests. She was arrested at one of them. And while they didn't exactly reverse US policy, they did make a difference. Our governor defied the Reagan administration by refusing to send the Massachusetts National Guard to conduct military exercises in Central America. Cambridge declared itself a sanctuary city for refugees from the conflict and chose as our sister city a Salvadoran village that had been devastated by violence; we sent medical supplies and other kinds of support.[5]

Around this time, my mom started learning Spanish and traveling to Central America whenever she could. She went to Guatemala, El Salvador, Honduras. She went mainly to get a better sense of what was happening there and to bring the news back home to help strengthen the case against further US intervention. A lot of activists believed that if American citizens were on the ground in these countries, our government wouldn't risk their lives by invading.

She brought me along on three of the tamer trips. To start with, we'd live with local families and take language classes, and then we'd spend the rest of the trip backpacking around the country, riding on buses filled with chickens. The summer we went to Guatemala, there was still fighting going on up in the mountains. Once, a truck passed me with a bunch of kids in the back. They had camo paint on their faces and guns in their hands. They were on their way to join the battle in the hills. I was seventeen at the time, and they looked like they were around my age or even younger. I'll never forget making eye contact with one of them and seeing his blank stare. That kid had seen a lot of things I hadn't and never would.

The next summer—it was 1989 and I'd just finished my first year of college—my mom said: "Matt, I've been restraining myself on these trips because you and Kyle need a mom. But you're both grown now, and you should know I'm not going to do that anymore." She started going to more dangerous places—including Cambridge's sister city in El Salvador. The town had been suspected of harboring guerrillas, and while she was there, the Salvadoran army came in, fired their guns in the air, and urinated in the town well to contaminate the water. Thankfully my mom was unhurt. She came home even more intent on engaging with the world—on working to figure out what was going on, and how she could take a more active role in righting injustices.

But her views on all this were complicated. As determined as she was to make a difference, she was also deeply skeptical of people, governments, aid organizations—anyone, really— rushing into struggling communities in the name of help. I remember her telling me that intervention—however well-meaning it might be—can come from a place of condescension, can even reflect a kind of unconscious racism, an assumption that black and brown people just aren't capable of helping themselves. She couldn't stand the arrogance of relief workers who thought they had it all figured out, who just needed to bestow their wisdom and largesse on people in need. (Seriously, don't get her started on this.)

My mom turned this scrutiny on herself, too. She knew her heart was in the right place, but she also knew that wasn't enough. Her travels showed her how hard it was to truly understand the complexities of life in a country where you've never lived, to appreciate a set of circumstances so different from any you've ever faced, or to anticipate the consequences of any ideas you bring from the outside. The caricature of the crusading liberal is pretty familiar. But it was clear to me that my mom wasn't crusading. She was wrestling—with herself and her own hesitations. She was working hard to avoid the traps she saw all around her. She was trying to be humble, never presumptuous, trying to make sure she never imagined, even subconsciously, that she knew more about the circumstances of these Salvadorans or Mexicans or Guatemalans than they did themselves. And so, armed with self-awareness, at least, she got back on a plane to see what she could do.

But a lot of time—years, actually—passed between having those conversations with my mom and applying those lessons myself. They were years in which, for a while, I was living out of a duffel bag, going from friends' couches to acting jobs and back to friends' couches—years in which engaging with the world, to be honest, took a back seat to getting bigger and better roles and steady work. Then, when that began to happen, it took all my energies to make sure it kept on happening; then Lucy and I were starting a family, and so on; and before I knew it, it was 2006, and Bono was pestering me to get involved. He had shown that advocating for others didn't mean you had to stop living your own life. He and U2 didn't stop recording albums during all those years he'd been campaigning against poverty. He didn't quit his day job or give any less of himself to his wife, Ali, and their four kids.

And he didn't hang back out of concern that people were going to roll their eyes every time a rich rock star started talking about poverty, or that they were going to call him a hypocrite or a dilettante or a photo-op philanthropist. People did call him all these things, and still do; it comes with the territory. But Bono takes the position that a little eye-rolling and some snark on social media is a small price to pay for doing *something* as opposed to, you know, doing nothing, or simply writing checks. Don't get me wrong: giving to charities is important, and if you've been lucky, as I've been, you can give something proportionate to the good fortune you've received. I've always been a big believer in that. But at the same time I had the feeling there was more I could be doing. That trip in 2006 was my first real step toward figuring out what that might be.

It wasn't immediately obvious to me that I should focus on water. The trip had been a blur. DATA had thrown so much at me so quickly that I was reeling; I had to spend some time sorting through it all and deciding where I might make a difference.

My first instinct was to focus on what seemed to be causing the most immediate suffering: HIV/AIDS. Early in the trip, we spent a day in Soweto, South Africa's largest township, to learn more about the HIV crisis. We went to meet two young boys—one around twelve years old, the other around seven—whose parents had died of AIDS. The boys were living on their own now, just the two of them. The older boy told me how he had to function as both parents to his little brother. One of the things that struck me was how spotless their room was. No one was there to clean it for them. No one was there to tell them to clean it. They just did it on their own.

I walked out and said: "What are these kids going to do? What's going to happen to them?" And our guides explained, matter-of-factly, that the boys would probably end up in gangs. They said that gangs in the city had all sorts of techniques to pull in desperate young boys who needed money. They usually succeeded.

I couldn't stop thinking about that moment for the rest of the trip. I wanted to do something to help combat the AIDS crisis, and there were clear opportunities to get involved—fighting AIDS was very much the focus of DATA. But the more I learned, the less confident I was that the war on AIDS needed me as a foot soldier. Thanks to activists around the world and leaders like Bono, Bill Gates, and former presidents Bill Clinton and George W. Bush, governments had belatedly gotten serious about stopping the spread of AIDS. Of course a lot more funding and support were needed. But other problems were causing a lot of pain, too, and getting just a fraction of the attention.

Education was an issue I connected with personally, given my upbringing, and I knew that the value of education was easy to communicate, since so many people, irrespective of background, have experienced it firsthand. But again, there was no shortage of people working on this issue. Then I thought I should channel my mom's example, and think about what the people I met on the trip asked me to work on. But that had happened to me just once. We were eating dinner at the home of the chief of a village outside Lusaka. All of a sudden, he leaned forward and asked: "When can we do something about the crocodiles?"

Turns out that in his village, crocodiles were killing more people than AIDS was. Needless to say, this wasn't in my briefing book. I asked one of the folks at DATA if there was something we could do, and she said she'd look into it. I guess the solution was pretty simple. It wasn't going to take a UN commission to figure it out: traps, guns, that sort of thing. Still, I couldn't imagine myself as the champion of that cause. *Matt Damon, Crocodile Hunter.*

My mind kept going back to that girl in blue and our walk to the well. And the more I thought about her situation, and about everything else I learned about water, the more I saw how central water is to everything. Life's impossible without it. And when clean water is unavailable, human progress is impossible.

Every other issue I encountered on the trip, or read about in the news, seemed to trace back to water. Health, for example. Diarrhea, the most common symptom of waterborne diseases, kills more children than malaria, measles, and HIV/AIDS—combined.[6] For millions more children, waterborne diseases cause such severe malnourishment that their physical and mental growth is stunted forever.[7] And there are even further health consequences for the women and girls who transport the water. As Åsa Regnér, the deputy executive director of UN Women, has put it: "All this fetching and carrying, usually from a young age, causes cumulative wear-and-tear to the neck, spine, back and knees. In effect, a woman's body becomes part of the water-delivery infrastructure, doing the work of pipes."[8]

Water is central to the fight to get more kids in school, too. Illnesses caused by waterborne diseases cause 443 million missed school days each year.[9] The lack of bathrooms and sanitary products keeps girls at home for multiple days each month when they have their menstrual cycles. And of course, the long walks to water cause girls to drop out completely. If you want kids in the classroom, you have to end the water crisis.

And if you're concerned about gender equity—what more significant step could we take to empower women and girls than simply to give them back their days?

The water crisis is also a big driver of extreme poverty, costing economies around the world $260 billion every year.[10] And as we're already seeing, water shortages are one of the most devastating consequences of a warming climate. For people who are connected to water infrastructure, shortages will be expensive. For people who aren't, shortages will be deadly.

"Water is the first principle of everything."[11] Thales, the ancient Greek philosopher, said that. It looked to me like Thales was right. Every other conversation I was having about development issues—health, education, women's rights, economic opportunity, the environment—could have started, maybe should have started, with a discussion of water. Or, to be exact, a discussion of WASH—the usual shorthand for water, sanitation, and hygiene, which are often treated as a single issue. But hardly anyone was talking about it. I kept coming back to something one of Bono's colleagues had told me. "Water is the least sexy of all causes," he said. *Yeah*, I thought. *Now try adding shit to it!*

Why are water and sanitation so unsexy—why do they get such little attention? Over the years I've developed and discarded a bunch of theories. The one I've hung on to is best captured by a parable David Foster Wallace once told:

> There are these two young fish swimming along and they happen to meet an older fish swimming the other way, who nods at them and says "Morning, boys. How's the water?" And the two young fish swim on for a bit, and then eventually one of them looks over at the other and goes "What the hell is water?"[12]

Wallace used the story to illustrate that, in his words, "the most obvious, important realities are often the ones that are hardest to see and talk about." But for me it's not just a metaphor. When it comes to water, it's almost literally true.

We are surrounded by water. We wake up and shower with water, brush our teeth with water, flush our toilet with water, make coffee with water, drink a glass of water, wash our dishes with water, all before we even leave the house. We never imagine we might have to go without it—because we never do. We rarely think about paying for it because it's so cheap it's virtually free, unless it's in a plastic bottle advertising its electrolytes. The one drink you get for free at any Starbucks, or any restaurant, is a glass of water. We're used to drinking for free from fountains, or using free bathrooms.

So you and me—we're the fish. "What the hell is water?"

Water and sanitation are so available to us that we don't notice them; we don't even see them. And except on rare occasions, like the devastating failure of the water system in Flint, Michigan, we're never without them. We know what it's like to skip a meal from time to time; we've seen an empty fridge. So we know what it might conceivably feel like to be hungry. But how many of us have ever turned on every faucet in our house, every tap in our whole town, and seen nothing come out? How many of us have even imagined that?

About twenty years ago, I read a story in the *LA Times* about two college roommates who'd gone on a road trip. They got out at Carlsbad Caverns, went out for a hike, and got lost. They were wandering around for four days with no water. The thirst was so agonizing that one of them begged his friend to kill him rather than let him die from dehydration. The friend had a small knife with him. And he actually did it—actually killed his best friend—only to learn, not long after, that they were just 240 feet off the trail.[13]

They did an autopsy on the kid, and it showed something surprising. He hadn't been dying of thirst. He hadn't been close to dying of thirst. He just hadn't realized what he was experiencing—because *he'd never been truly thirsty before.*

In 1906, a scientist named W. J. McGee interviewed a man who had survived for almost a week without water in the Arizona desert. McGee described thirst as having three stages. The first is normal dryness, which we all know. The second stage is where your throat burns, your skin tightens, and eventually you start going insane. The last stage is what McGee called "a progressive mummification" of the body.[14] The kid was somewhere in stage two.

I was so gripped and horrified by this story that the morning I read it, when the director Gus Van Sant called me about something else, I told him about it, and we ended up doing a movie based on it—a movie called *Gerry*. Okay, maybe not the most uplifting film I've ever made. Not really a date night thing. But I found it fascinating how fully we, in wealthy countries like ours, had lost touch with some of the most basic human experiences, like profound, sustained, even dangerous thirst.

Which is why, I think, it takes time for this issue to register with people. Sometimes I get frustrated when people don't just get it. Then I remember that I didn't, either. Even after I met Wema, who made such a vivid impression on me, the concept of chronic thirst and a lack of access to water was so foreign to me that it still took me awhile to grasp how much it was defining her life.

But in time I felt like I did get it—I understood the problem, if not its solutions. And I had a sense that this crisis would get the attention it needed once we got more people to hear stories like this girl's. And what is celebrity if not a totally needless surplus of attention? If I could redirect some of it toward a cause that needed it, I'd feel like I'd started, at least, to make some kind of difference.

And look—I'm not claiming I'm the best spokesperson for this issue. Let's just come out and say it: you're reading a book by two privileged white guys—about an issue that primarily affects marginalized black and brown people, and women especially. I'm speaking out because the only remedy I know to the problem that not enough people care about water is to keep talking about it myself.

But I know that getting involved in an issue that affects communities you are not a part of requires constant listening and learning. It requires awareness of your own assumptions and biases, deep humility about all the ways good work can go wrong, and a commitment to keep looking for ways to do it better. In other words, it takes that combination of thoughtfulness and fearlessness that my mom taught me all those years ago. I hope you'll hold me accountable to her example.

Not long before the Africa trip I happened to get involved in a documentary about three guys who'd decided to run across four thousand miles of the scorching sand of the Sahara Desert—all the way from the west, where the Atlantic Ocean meets Senegal, to the east, where Egypt meets the Red Sea.[15] I got talked into it by one of the runners, a charismatic guy named Charlie Engle. A few decades ago, Charlie woke up on a motel floor after a cocaine binge, almost dead. He got up, cleaned up, and started running. He never stopped. He took all his addictive tendencies and applied them to running; he became an ultramarathoner.

When I met Charlie, the two of us went on a ten-mile run, and he asked me if I'd ever run a marathon. I said I hadn't. "My brother runs marathons," I told him, "and I trained for one, but my Achilles tendons start to break down after about twelve miles."

"No they don't," he said.

As the owner of the tendons we were talking about, I disagreed. I said they did.

"They don't," he said again. Then this gem: "You need to reorient your relationship to pain."

If Charlie sounds like a barely credible movie character—he did to me, too. But I liked him, and I liked his project. I signed on as an executive producer and said I would narrate the film. I agreed to do it because I thought it was an interesting story— human beings against the elements, that sort of thing. But by the time the runners were ready to cross the continent and our crew went to Africa to film them, I saw it a little differently. By then I had been to parts of Africa with DATA, and when I looked at the route these runners were going to travel—through Senegal, Mauritania, Mali, Niger, Libya, and Egypt—the map looked to me like Ground Zero in the global water crisis. Here were countries facing extreme water shortages—and lacking the infrastructure to address the problem. If you wanted to understand or to do something about the water crisis, this was a good place to start.

While preparing to shoot the film, I learned that there were organizations doing great work to get the people of the region access to water and sanitation. These groups were short on funding, though, and it occurred to me that this was something I could do: raise money. So I talked with the others who were leading the project, and we decided to create a charitable arm for the expedition: the H_2O Africa Foundation.

We knew it was going to take a lot of work to identify the best water and sanitation organizations, learn about their work, vet them to see if they'd make good partners, and fund them. Fortunately, because of the film, we were going to have people on the ground, moving across the area. I don't mean the runners. They had enough to worry about, like surviving. I mean the people who were following the runners in cars and trucks, helping in various ways and recording the journey. Along the way, they'd have a chance to speak with locals about their water challenges, and keep an eye out for organizations that were helping.

To understand how incredible an opportunity that was, know that just getting into some of these countries is tricky. Even as the runners were in Niger, making their way across the desert there, Libya—which shares a border to the northeast—hadn't approved their application to enter the country. I was shooting *The Bourne Ultimatum* at the time, and I ended up flying from the set in Europe to Washington, DC, to try to convince some officials at the Libyan embassy to let the runners in. Clearly, I'm not as charming as I like to think, because their answer was no. It took a Libyan-born businessman pulling some strings to get the application approved.[16]

So it was a big win just to have people in these countries in the first place, and I wanted to make the most of the opportunity. Of course, I knew that doing this research on the side, while shooting a movie, was a highly imperfect approach. When you get a degree in, say, development studies at, say, the London School of Economics, this is not what they teach you. But I wasn't getting a degree in development studies. I was making a documentary, and I was eager to kick-start my own learning process. I kept coming back to a line on a magnet that my mom kept on our fridge when I was growing up. It was a quote widely attributed to Gandhi: "Whatever you do may seem insignificant to you, but it is most important that you do it."

And I'm glad we did. The team identified some amazing organizations doing indispensable work—and they were reminded every day of how much more work needed to be done. Once, while the crew was driving along in a truck loaded with water and food for the runners, they came across a seven-year-old boy sitting alone, obviously scared, in the desert. He had a little camel milk with him, and a little dried meat, but that was all. His parents had left him there while they went to collect water—a journey that, in the heart of the Sahara, took two full days, and required two people. The family owned a herd of sheep, goats, and a camel—and their only option was to leave the boy alone, tending to the animals. The crew asked him if this happened often. He said it did. They gave him a box of cookies, a bag of fresh dates, and a few big bottles of water, but they knew that none of this was a lasting solution—that as their truck drove away, sending up clouds of sand, they would quickly seem, to the boy, like a surreal sort of dream.[17]

The runners and the crew kept hearing a phrase in the local language, Tamashek: *Aman iman.*

"Water is life."[18]

H_2O Africa raised a pretty good sum through the movie and its promotion; then money from other sources started coming in. OneXOne, a Canadian charity that invests in organizations that promote children's well-being, donated a million dollars to H_2O Africa when I hosted a gala for them in Toronto. Then we got a major grant from the PepsiCo Foundation, which invests heavily in partnerships to help end the water crisis. It felt like a major vote of confidence in what we were doing.

The more success we had in raising money—and redirecting it to organizations on the ground in Africa—the more aware I became of the gaps in my knowledge, in my experience. Success in fundraising carries a responsibility to be a good steward of the resources that people entrust to you—which meant that I had a lot more learning to do. I'd been happy to get started without having total command of the facts. But I wasn't okay continuing that way.

I started reading more about the crisis and meeting with experts. I'd long admired the economist Jeffrey Sachs, who is a major player in development circles and, I had heard, a big influence on Bono's thinking. (Bono calls himself a "Jeff Sachs groupie.") I first met Jeff at the gala in Toronto, and he became an incredible mentor to me, always willing to meet for long lunches and help me start to understand—if not fluently speak—the language of development. Here, by the way, is a warning. If and when you try to learn about a great global challenge like water, be aware that many of the sentences you encounter are going to read like this: "Managing water resources involves a dialectic between integration (Dublin Principle 1) and subsidiarity (Dublin Principle 2)."[19]

When this happens, back away slowly from the website. Just don't give up. Seriously, almost every major player in the development world speaks in jargon like this. A lot of it, I think, is just the shorthand that develops among experts. Hollywood has its own version: "tent poles," "beat sheets," "slug lines." Whatever industry you're part of, impenetrable language is a kind of gatekeeping. If nothing else, it communicates: "We know a lot about this, and you don't." Which of course is completely true—the experts are always going to know way more than you; that's why they're experts and you, with all due respect, are not. I'm not, either.

And I'm okay with that. I'm more than willing to feel less than smart, to ask questions that expose me as clueless or at least a little naïve. Turns out I'm better at this than I expected. But there does come a point—and for H_2O Africa, it came a couple of years after we started—when it's no longer enough to be a willing student. What I came to realize was that I didn't need a teacher; I needed a partner—someone who knew more about water than I ever would but might be willing to join forces and do more as a team than either of us could do on our own. I still didn't know much, but I had learned enough to know there was one guy who seemed to know water better than anyone else. And that was Gary White.

2

THE WATER DECADE

POV: Gary White

Let me start by saying that I'm not the kind of guy you'd expect to walk out on one of his first desk jobs. It's probably important for me to make that clear—before I tell you about the time I did exactly that.

When *Esquire* ran one of the early profiles of Water.org in 2009, the reporter who accompanied us on a field visit to India explained the difference between Matt and me by describing our outfits—which at first glance seemed exactly the same. We were both wearing button-down shirts and khakis, except Matt's shirt was loose and untucked, its top few buttons undone. Mine was tucked in and cinched by a belt. I had a ballpoint pen in my shirt pocket. "The effect," the reporter wrote, "is night and day, black and white, movie star and engineer."[1]

He wasn't wrong. I often come across as a buttoned-up engineer, even when I'm not standing next to Matt Damon for contrast.

Suffice it to say that I'm not the type for dramatic gestures. That's what made that day in the winter of 1989 so strange. I'd just moved to Denver to take a job at an engineering consulting firm. My job was to design a pipeline that would carry water from one place in Pueblo, Colorado, to another place in Pueblo, Colorado. It wasn't glamorous work, but it was important, in its way.

So in the middle of my second week on the job, when I stood up at my desk and walked out of the office and down the street, it wasn't an act of protest. It didn't even feel like a conscious choice. I was just restless. Not in a get-up-and-stretch-your-legs sort of way. I mean restless in an existential sense. I just needed to walk, to get some space to think.

A few months earlier, I'd been wandering around the Guatemalan Highlands as an engineering specialist for Catholic Relief Services. My job was to oversee projects that CRS was supporting across Latin America and the Caribbean. But that didn't count toward the professional engineering license I was pursuing. For that, I needed another year of officially approved engineering experience. Hence the job in Denver.

Most of the projects I'd been supervising at CRS were water projects. In the villages I'd visited, I met women whose entire lives, every minute of every day, were shaped by the fact that they didn't have access to water and sanitation—from the moment they woke up (often at 4:00 a.m. so they could go to the bathroom in the fields while it was still dark, and therefore a little more private), to the daytime hours they spent collecting water, to the nights when they went to bed covered in grime because they had only enough water to wash their children.

Compare that with my new job. Most of the people in Pueblo, Colorado, never thought about water at all, and it was my job to make sure they didn't have to—to ensure that at the touch of a handle, the toilet flushed away the waste, and the faucets and showers and hoses ran clean. It was a worthy thing to be doing. But it felt to me like doing yardwork while your neighbor's house was on fire.

Without realizing it, I'd walked for miles. I hadn't been paying attention to where I was going, but somehow I'd ended up at my church. I went inside to sit down for a while. The building was deserted. I found a spot in a pew and debated whether or not to quit my job.

This church was relatively new to me since I'd just moved to town, but it reminded me of home. Growing up in Kansas City, Missouri, I lived a block from St. Bernadette's, our local Catholic church, and went to Mass every Sunday. I also went to a Catholic high school run by the Christian Brothers order, even though the cost of the tuition made it a luxury for us. My parents couldn't afford it for my three older siblings, but they told me if I found a way to pay half my tuition, they would cover the rest. During the summer, to help pay my share, I worked as a janitor at the St. Bernadette's grade school, mopping the same floors and cleaning the same toilets I thought I'd left behind when I graduated.

In school and in church, I was taught: "Unless a life is lived for others, it's not worth living." My parents—particularly my mom, Kathy White—took that teaching to heart. She'd grown up on a Missouri farm and migrated to the big city in the late 1940s, so she never had the same chance I would get to serve others halfway around the world. But she still led a life of service. When she wasn't at home dedicating her life to her five kids, she was a block up the hill at the church, donating her time. She helped to resettle Vietnamese refugees and raised funds to support people in poverty in Kansas City. Our church, like most churches, had rummage sales to raise money to donate, and my mom would be there every day, sorting through piles of clothing and old toys.

So service had always been important to me. But sitting in that church in Denver, I thought about the phrase that Catholics often use, a phrase that happened to be the title of a class I had taken in high school: "Social Justice." Of course social justice can mean many things, but for me it brought to mind a moment from the first volunteer trip I'd taken abroad, back in college. I was in the slums of Guatemala City, where I saw a little girl, maybe five or six years old, filling a bucket from a filthy barrel of water. Her bucket must have weighed almost as much as she did. She heaved it up, put it on her head, and teetered home along a stream of sewage. I wanted to free her from that heavy load, as anyone would; I wanted to find a way to communicate that this water could make her very sick or even kill her. But I couldn't. My Spanish at that point was too poor to explain the risk. And in any case, this was the only water she was going to get, because she had been born into poverty in the wrong place.

It wasn't just sad. It wasn't just tragic. It was an injustice— a word I knew not to use lightly. In that moment in Guatemala City, I understood something that before I had only studied, had only known in the abstract: that for billions of people like this little girl, every day is a struggle to meet their most basic needs. For them, making sure that their families have water to drink and food to eat and a safe place to sleep takes so much of their energy that they have nothing left to invest in their own future. So generations of people, through no fault of their own, stay trapped in this desperate loop. My upbringing taught me that the world didn't have to be this way—*that we could choose for it not to be this way*—but we don't, so it is.

I needed to quit.

If this was a novel, I would never have walked back to that desk again. But as I said, I'm not a dramatic guy. I called in sick for the rest of the day—and the next. And I was sick, emotionally speaking. (I was also painfully sunburned after wandering around all day in the sun.) I made a plan with my wife, Becky: I'd stay at the Denver job long enough to take the professional engineer exam—and not a day longer, even if I failed it. I'd also apply to grad school so I could keep learning about water and exploring new ways I could help address the crisis.

I followed the plan. I was accepted into a master's program in environmental engineering at UNC Chapel Hill, home of some of the world's leading water experts. And not long after my one-year anniversary at the consulting firm, I gave my employer two weeks' notice.

◊

I decided to organize a water-focused fundraiser at St. Bernadette's. I called it the Thanksgiving Water Dinner because that was when it took place: late November 1990. We raised money for Cocepradil, a fantastic organization in Honduras that works with communities to build spring-fed water systems. Our goal was to raise enough to help Cocepradil bring clean water to a community called El Limon. Like most Thanksgiving celebrations, this was a family affair: everyone in my extended family helped set up the dinner. My mom cornered everyone she knew after Mass, recruiting them to come. She was our first and most effective volunteer. Thanks largely to her, a hundred of our friends and family turned up—way more than I'd expected. Meissen's Catering, a local business run by a friend of the family, donated the meals, and I put on a slideshow of water projects from my time at Catholic Relief Services. I was lucky that Father Pat Tobin, a wonderful Kansas City priest whom Mother Teresa had asked to lead retreats for her Sisters of Charity in India, offered to speak. That night, we raised over $4,000. Becky made a banner for everyone at the dinner to sign. The next year, when I visited El Limon to see how the project was progressing, I presented it to the community.

The dinner was such a success that we decided to host it again in Kansas City the next year, and to host one in Chapel Hill as well. Some of my engineering classmates stepped up to form a committee—especially my good friend Marla Smith, who stood out as the most committed volunteer. The two of us registered a new organization: the International Partnership for Safe Water, or IPSW. (We're engineers. Branding isn't our strong suit.) A few of our engineering professors formed IPSW's first board.

I was excited about the road ahead. But I was also aware that starting an organization to address the global water crisis in the early 1990s was like showing up at a party just as everyone is packing up and heading home.

Many people have forgotten this by now, or are too young to know or remember, but the 1980s were a time of great hope in the water and sanitation world. The period had been designated by the United Nations as the International Drinking Water Supply and Sanitation Decade. (UN officials aren't great at branding, either.) The UN made that choice after hosting countless conferences on development issues in the sixties and seventies and discovering that no matter the theme—overpopulation or urbanization or the environment—the conversation always seemed to come back to water. Lack of water was one of the greatest challenges facing developing nations: only 40 percent of people had access to safe drinking water, and only 25 percent had access to even the most basic forms of sanitation.[2] Every year, lack of safe drinking water killed an estimated 15 million children.[3]

As developing nations called attention to the crises they were facing, it became increasingly clear that healthy societies need clean, accessible water as urgently as our own bodies do. So, in 1980, the UN General Assembly set a goal that by the end of the decade, everyone everywhere would have access to safe water and sanitation.

I'd started working at Catholic Relief Services in the middle of the Water Decade, and I felt excited to be a part of the effort. I was brand new to this work, so it was no surprise that I was feeling idealistic, but even the experts seemed to be saying the world could solve the water crisis—if not by 1990, which most people saw as a highly ambitious target, then maybe by the following decade.

Honestly, back then I had a pretty idealized vision of what it would take to end the crisis—and what my role in that would be. I remember thinking that to be as efficient as possible, I'd get my pilot's license and fly myself to places that needed engineering help to get clean water.

It wasn't long before I was set straight. As I visited villages across Latin America in dire need of clean water, I started to see something that, at first, made no sense at all: state-of-the-art wells, recently built, already broken down and abandoned.

The core of the problem was that most of these water and sanitation projects weren't being built *with* the local community. They were being built *for* the local community.

In those days, many of the US government programs brought in American firms to design water projects and American firms to supply the materials. At the United States Agency for International Development, this was actually mandated. During the Water Decade, US law required that USAID use American contractors for most development work—the logic being that if we're going to help all these people, we might as well get something out of it, too. Even into the 2000s, the US government saw this as a virtue, not a problem. USAID publicity materials used to boast: "The principal beneficiary of America's foreign assistance programs has always been the United States. Close to 80% of the US Agency for International Development's contracts and grants go directly to American firms."[4]

In theory, the approach is win-win—help yourself by helping others. But it didn't work that way in practice. (A former USAID director admitted that these rules, set by Congress, were his "biggest headache" at the agency.)[5] Because just drilling a well isn't enough. The well, by design, is going to be in constant use, and at some point, some part is going to break. And if that well has been installed by an American firm, using American-made parts—how is the local community going to fix it? Unless that community knows where to get a replacement part, and has been collecting maintenance fees from everyone so they can special-order that part from overseas, and is then able to install that part, what they're eventually going to have is a nonworking well. That likelihood was largely overlooked at the time, especially in the rush to get these wells installed.

So many of the wells simply broke down—and stayed that

way. Researchers studied these water projects two to five years after they were completed—and found that between 30 percent and 50 percent of them had broken down.[6]

Some of the wells that did keep working were bringing up seriously contaminated water. After I got sick from drinking water in Guatemala, I designed the first water quality research test that Catholic Relief Services had ever conducted. I'll never forget trying to get all my testing equipment and chemicals (including flammables) onto the plane with me. I kept trying to explain to security that I needed all this stuff in order to assess the quality of water in the Dominican Republic. They looked at me like I was insane, but they let me on board.

The results of many of those tests were shocking. Typically, to measure the level of contamination of a water supply, you collect about 100 milliliters of that water, put it on a filter, let the bacteria grow, and then count the bacteria colonies you see. This gives you a rough sense of how toxic your water is. But if it's badly contaminated, you won't even be able to distinguish the individual colonies from one another. In that case, what you write in your report is "TNTC": too numerous to count. There were a lot of TNTCs in our report.

But even the best-case scenario—a well that works and brings up clean water—doesn't do much good if a community hasn't been taught how to keep water clean. We learn during childhood (and we had the lesson reinforced during the COVID-19 pandemic) that germs spread disease; we learn that washing your hands gets rid of those germs; yet despite all that, we've all been in public restrooms and seen people walk out without washing. Imagine how much worse it would be if nobody in your community had that knowledge about germs, and if there were no sinks at all. The horrible irony of these habits is that clean water that had come at such great expense was being contaminated just as soon as it was drawn from the well.

Many of the new toilets were a bust, too. Pit latrines are often dark, small, enclosed spaces—and as you can imagine, they don't smell very good. It's kind of counterintuitive that a place that's so smelly can also be more sanitary. For many people, going to the bathroom out in the open air actually feels cleaner. So if no one explains that it can lead to disease, that it can cause human waste to get into the water supply, pit latrines will often go unused.

At the beginning of the Water Decade, there'd been a lot of talk about community engagement. However, truly engaging with the community, not just talking with people but really listening to them, takes work—especially if the project is being led by someone who lives in another country. And the Water Decade had started a rush to get these wells installed. Even though most water and sanitation nongovernmental organizations (NGOs) in these areas did a bit of hygiene education, we could see that it wasn't reaching many people. In my work for CRS, I'd knock on doors and ask when the health worker last visited their house. And they'd say: "What health worker?"

Some organizations had begun to face up to these problems while others could get pretty defensive. Even if they didn't say it directly, you got the sense that they were telling themselves:

Well, we did some good. We improved some people's lives. Shouldn't that be enough?

And on a certain level, that's understandable. But once you began thinking about the water crisis as a massive affront to social justice that the world was urgently responsible for addressing, then it just wasn't enough.

Later on, I'd learn that this way of thinking is what separates what we now call social entrepreneurs from those who use traditional models of charitable investment: social entrepreneurs constantly take stock of their efforts relative to their goals, always evaluating whether their solutions are matching what the problem requires. And if they can't answer yes, they move quickly to develop new solutions. But the term *social entrepreneur* hadn't yet been coined.

I left CRS for that job in Denver in 1989, just as the Water Decade was drawing to a close. Looking back the year after the Water Decade concluded, a leader at the World Bank said that the effort had "bequeathed to the world a glass of water half full and half empty."[7] There were certainly successes to celebrate: thanks to increased attention and smarter investment, 1.3 billion people who lacked access to clean water in 1980 had it by 1990, and 750 million had access to toilets for the first time.[8] That's safe drinking water for an additional 360,000 people per day and sanitation for an additional 205,000 people per day. For all the joking people do about UN-declared days and months and years and decades (mark your calendar for World Tuna Day, May 2), it really can make a difference to declare a common goal and rally around it.

But for all this success, in 1990 there were still 1.2 billion people who lacked access to clean water, compared with 1.8 billion in 1980. And there were 1.7 billion who lacked access to a toilet—*almost exactly the same number as in 1980*. How could that be? What we came to understand was that our efforts were just barely keeping pace with population growth. It's ironic, even perverse, but we were making progress without gaining ground. Governments didn't have the funds to increase their efforts. The "Buy America" rule generated a lot of waste, since it required shipping expensive parts and buying expensive plane tickets to fly in expensive American engineers. And other global problems were driving up costs: industrialization's mounting damage to the environment made clean water harder and more costly to find, and in the early 1980s, the global economy saw a downturn that left many governments and NGOs with fewer resources to spend on water and sanitation.

We had every reason to expect that the population would continue to grow, and the wells that the world had spent a decade building would continue breaking down just as the attention and funding the UN had directed toward the water crisis dried up. The Water Decade had been the start of something. But it also seemed, by 1990, like the end of something.

Someone needed to figure out a new strategy to combat the crisis. And maybe it was a bit audacious for our little baby NGO to think we'd be the ones to step in and change the way this work was done, but I've always tended to plunge into solving problems—trying to solve them, anyway—without dwelling on all the challenges that might lie ahead. I'd figured out that if you want to make a change in this world, you just do what you have to do to get over the hurdle in front of you, and once you've done that and can see the next hurdle, you start figuring out a way to get over that.

I first learned this lesson long ago, back in high school, when administrators cut our soccer program. I was despondent. I had no idea how to reverse their decision, but I went to work on it regardless. I put together a plan and budget and somehow managed to get on the agenda of the school board to make my pitch. They agreed—the first hurdle was passed! But they gave us no funding for a new coach. So I coached the team my senior year. It's remarkable how much playing time you can get when you are the coach.

Later on, in college, I learned that a former campus minister from my school had created a program at another university that sent students on service trips around the world—trips to build water systems, schools, and health facilities. But the construction efforts proved to be a challenge because these were all liberal arts students; they needed some engineering expertise. So I created the Student Engineering Network for International Technical Assistance (SENITA). (I should have asked the liberal arts students to come up with a name.) I recruited other students to apply, professors to advise us, and engineering firms to sponsor our efforts. That Guatemala trip I mentioned happened only because of SENITA.

I didn't appreciate the dangers of what we were getting into. In Guatemala, I was chased by a pack of stray dogs and got bitten. Rabies shots were required. Then, the day I was flying home, a plane in Guatemala crashed. Members of my family were beside themselves until they learned it wasn't my plane. My mom implemented a policy: Whenever I got back to college safely, I was to make a person-to-person call home and ask for Chester. She'd say he couldn't talk, so the operator would disconnect us. Consequently, I was not charged for the call, but the message was sent and received: I was safe. And she didn't have to lie: Chester could never talk, because he was the family dog.

In the end, no students were injured in the making of SENITA, and the work was a big success—I was even interviewed by the local newspaper and the local TV station about the program. So by the time I started IPSW, it had been ingrained in me that the best way to take on a big problem is to not let myself get intimidated by it, and just get to work.

We started crafting a new strategy to combat the crisis at IPSW—which, in a flash of either inspiration or common sense, we soon renamed WaterPartners. We didn't choose the name just because it sounded friendlier. Partnership—specifically with local organizations that built water systems—became the core of our strategy. Our partners were the on-the-ground, home-grown experts in how to tap local water sources, how to design water systems that could be maintained by the community, and how to talk to people about hygiene in ways that broke through.

Of course, it's not like we came up with the idea of partnering with local organizations. But many of the partnerships between water and sanitation NGOs and local water organizations were more like flings than lasting relationships. The donors and the NGOs weren't putting in the enormous effort it took to rigorously evaluate the best local partners, and, perhaps inevitably, the partnerships didn't last very long. Either the local partner would fall short on execution or the supporting NGO would come across some exciting new project and redirect its funding there, leaving local partners hanging.

So WaterPartners was more focused than probably any other NGO in the sector on identifying the best local partners and collaborating closely with them over the long haul. Our evaluation process was extremely competitive—we vetted about twenty of these groups for every one we decided to work with. But once you became one of our certified partners, you'd stay one, as long as you kept doing effective work.

Once we found a local partner, we'd work with them to design a water system that was as simple as possible. Whether we were drilling a well, constructing a piped system, or harvesting rainwater, we relied on hand pumps or gravity, rather than complicated electric pumps, to move the water. We used local materials and local workers so that when problems cropped up, they knew how to fix them. And we worked with the community to make sure they elected a water board to manage the well and knew how to collect water fees—usually called water tariffs—from everyone in the community so that the system could be maintained.

To many people, "community engagement" sounds like a fuzzy, feel-good thing, but we took it very seriously. I remember attending a festival in a town in Haiti—sort of an inaugural ceremony for a water system that our partner had helped build. A big spread of refreshments had been set out; a marching band was playing. We and our partners huddled with the leaders of the project and hit them with the usual questions: Who was going to collect the fees from the citizens? Where was that money going to be kept? Was there a bank account? In most cases community leaders had answers to these questions, but in this case, the response was silence. We asked about the system itself: Who here knows how to operate the valves? Again, no answer.

It was an awkward moment. (Actually, to be honest, it was a terrible moment.) Part of me felt like the compassionate thing to do was to let the ceremony go on, save everyone the embarrassment, and do damage control later. But as I stood there thinking about it, I felt that celebrating a water system that we knew was going to fail—that was not going to fulfill its promise to the community—was not an act of compassion, it was an act of condescension, as if hurt feelings mattered more than clean water. Clearly, we, the community leaders, and our local partners had more work to do. So after we huddled for a few minutes, our partners had the uncomfortable task of telling everyone that the opening was going to be delayed. They sent the band home.

It was a tough moment. I still wince thinking about it. But it was the right call. I spent a lot of time reflecting on what I'd allowed to slip through the cracks, and I resolved to be even more thorough going forward.

Thankfully, we didn't have to deal with situations like that very often. As I've mentioned, as few as 50 percent of water projects are successful in the long term.[9] At WaterPartners, our rate was higher than 90 percent. So most of the water project openings I went to were full of joy—and the happiness far outlasted the inaugural party. For families in these communities, life changed fundamentally. Women got their days back, days in which they could work, and not just carry water. More girls got to go to school. Fewer children died needlessly of waterborne diseases.

There was simple joy, too, in water itself. When a community finally has a clean source of water, when water feels safe and no longer scarce, you see people, hesitantly at first, splash a little on their faces to cool down, splash it at each other for fun, let it run through their hands—wondering at it, thrilling to it. Something that had always been associated with stress and disease and even death was suddenly a source of refreshment and relief.

For celebrations like these, I'd bring along a banner my wife had made. She'd written WaterPartners' slogan in Spanish: *DEL AGUA PROVIENE LA VIDA.*

"From water springs life."

I knew that getting easy access to water would transform these communities. But I was surprised to see that the process of constructing these water projects did, too. Because, again, these projects weren't the work of, say, American engineers parachuting in, clearing a space, drilling a well, and moving on. These projects were a community effort in the truest sense. With our support, the gravity-flow water systems were built and run by the communities themselves, requiring neighbors to come together and work together for their collective benefit. That sense of shared obligation and shared opportunity is something I wish I saw more often in the United States. Because these were not just water projects. They were democracy in its purest form. For many of the people in these towns, selecting the members of the water board was the first time they'd ever voted.

The availability of clean water changed the patterns of life in these communities in more ways than we could measure (as much as engineers like to measure). One of the most important, and inspiring, was the change we saw in the role of women. A lack of clean water always affects the women in the community the most. Its impact on their lives is an indignity and, even more, an injustice. It robs women of their agency and power: knowledge, as the saying goes, is power, and a lack of clean water was keeping them out of school, keeping them from learning. Money, too, brings power, and a lack of clean water was keeping them from earning an income. But the arrival of a clean water source had, in some wonderful ways, turned the situation on its head. Because water was thought to be *women's* business, women ended up on many of these water boards, even chairing some— which gave them authority over the community's most vital resource. Some women would form public health groups and ensure that water kept flowing. They were drawing power from what had once taken it from them, and when you talked to them, you couldn't miss the change in their demeanor. I'll never forget asking a community group, run entirely by women, if they'd allow a man to attend one of their meetings.

"Yes, of course," they told me. "If he's quiet and sits in the back."

I was thrilled with WaterPartners' progress. But there was always one big thing getting in its way: money.

I was always a lot more comfortable with doing the work than going out and talking about the work. For me, giving speeches and interviews was nerve-wracking. Standing up to ask people to give us their hard-earned money was even tougher. But I knew I couldn't opt out. Funding, for an NGO, is an existential issue. So whenever I needed to gather some courage, I'd always think back to one of my favorite quotes: "Evil flourishes when good people do nothing." That gave me the motivation I needed to keep speaking out, and over the years, I started getting better at it.

We'd grown slowly at first—expanding the dinners in Kansas City and Chapel Hill to various cities across the United States, and sending mailers asking for further donations. As we started getting good results, we courted larger investors, like foundations. Once, a single donor wrote us a check for

$25,000. I couldn't believe it. It was five times what we'd raised the year before.

With funding coming in, we were able to professionalize. We built our first headquarters, though this might have been putting it a little grandly: our so-called headquarters was a second-story addition on the house where Becky and I lived in Chapel Hill. Still, it felt like an office. And when I say *we* built it, I don't mean a contractor. One Saturday, we got a team of volunteers together, cut half the roof off our house, and framed in the office. I also got a salary: $100 a month. And we made a website, since the internet was now a thing. On a whim I registered a domain name I thought cut straight to the point: water.org.

By 1998, WaterPartners had raised $250,000. For someone who'd chased down every dollar, it felt like a lot. The easiest way to boost our funding further would have been to apply for government grants. But I never wanted to go down that path. Maybe I was just disillusioned with the water and sanitation development world as I'd come to see it back in the 1980s. It felt to me that taking those grants would require us to keep following other people's instructions, however misguided they might be, instead of searching for better ways of doing things. I wanted WaterPartners to own its future, so we kept searching for private donors.

The person who delivered one of our biggest breaks had just experienced her own: the singer Jewel. Yes, *that* Jewel—the singer of "Who Will Save Your Soul," who, in the mid-1990s, had one of the best-selling debut albums of all time. Jewel grew up in Alaska in a house with no running water and an outhouse in the back. I learned about Jewel's interest in water and sanitation from Marla, who reached out to her. Jewel agreed to meet with us, and over time we built a great relationship with her organization, The Clearwater Project. Eventually she committed $400,000 to WaterPartners over the course of three years. We were hugely grateful for it. Steady funding like that is a lifeline for an NGO—it means you can plan ahead and invest intelligently.

Then Napster happened. If we'd hired a management consultant (and we didn't) to assess the biggest threats to our budget, there's not a chance in the world that a music-piracy website would have made the list. But when Napster allowed people to download music for free, the whole music industry was upended, a lot of artists got hurt, and suddenly Jewel's money—and our Jewel money—was gone. Napster, it turned out, didn't just disrupt the music business. It blew a giant hole in the budget of a small NGO. It forced me to get in my old station wagon and drive around the country, taking old donors to dinner and begging them to re-up their commitments.

The woman who ultimately filled the Napster gap was Wynette LaBrosse, who'd founded a tech company named Finisar with her husband. On my fundraising road tour, someone set up a dinner with Wynette in Palo Alto, and she made a commitment that covered the loss from Jewel and then some.

Soon enough, though, that funding dried up, too.

Then the Michael and Susan Dell Foundation stepped in and made our biggest investment yet.

Tech giveth, tech taketh away, tech giveth again.

But even as donations grew over the years, they never felt like enough. There were always so many great projects waiting to get started, so many projects that could change lives now, so many projects we were desperate to fund—but we couldn't, because we didn't have the cash.

Back then I looked at that as a WaterPartners problem. If we could up our fundraising game, I thought, we could fix it. And certainly I could have been a better pitchman. But now, I see that the difficulty I had was emblematic of a funding challenge that was much larger than that, and much larger than we even understood.

Today's best estimates say that solving the water crisis would take $114 billion a year for ten years.[10] Right now, the total development assistance going to water and sanitation is just over $28.4 billion a year. Which means that over the next decade, we're on track to come up half a *trillion* dollars short.[11]

As the *New York Times* writer David Bornstein once put it, trying to solve the water crisis through charity well projects is "like using an 'adopt-a-highway' approach to solve the world's transportation problems."[12] In other words, good luck.

It's easy to feel defeated when you realize that your approach is destined to fail. But it's also kind of exciting. It forces you to look at a familiar problem from a new angle. It opens you up for a breakthrough.

3

THE BIG IDEA

POV: Gary White

As an engineer, I was hardwired to think that big break-throughs come from some new technological advance. But mine didn't. The breakthrough that would upend everything I thought I knew about the water crisis came on a field visit to Hyderabad, India, in 2003, as I was talking to a woman in a slum.

I hate that I've forgotten her name. At the time, I didn't re-alize the significance of the moment. But I can still picture her. She was elderly—in her seventies if I had to guess—and you could tell that movement was often painful for her. The slum where she'd built her shack was on a rocky hillside—so craggy and steep that it had clearly intimidated formal developers.

When you looked at them from far away, the shacks appeared as if they were stacked on top of one another.

There were no public toilets in the slum, and few people had them in their homes. So in order to keep the sewage away from their houses, the custom was for people in the community to walk down the hill to relieve themselves near the train tracks at its base.

Men would make the trip throughout the day, whenever they felt the need. But the women in the community were more concerned about privacy, partly out of fear. India ranks first in the world for the prevalence of sexual violence against women and third for nonsexual violence, and Indian women who lack access to toilets are more than twice as likely to be sexually assaulted by a stranger.[1, 2] So women usually went to relieve themselves only under cover of darkness—even though it often meant holding it throughout the day, and limiting the amount of food and water they consumed so they wouldn't have to go as badly. Then, in the middle of the night, they'd climb down the hill, with no streetlamps or flashlights to illuminate their path among the rocks.

This would be dangerous for anyone. But for the woman I met, it also meant physical pain. Her body was simply no longer up to the task. So she'd gotten a toilet installed in her house. I asked her how she'd managed that—toilets tend to cost a couple hundred dollars to install in India, and it's rare for people living in poverty to have that kind of money saved up. She explained she'd gotten a loan, and she told me how much it cost her every month to pay it back.

I did the math to calculate her interest rate. Then I went back and did the math again. I thought there had to be some mistake. I'd gotten a loan some years before to buy a house. The interest rate was about 5 percent. This woman had gotten a tiny loan, a mere fraction of the size of my home loan. But her interest rate was *125 percent*.

How was that possible? With no real trouble at all, I was able to get fair financing for a house that came with three full bathrooms—but this woman, who wanted only a single toilet so she could end her daily suffering, could not find, as I did, a financial institution that would lend her what she needed. She'd been left to the loan sharks.

On the flight home, I kept thinking: people who worked in water and sanitation—me included—were seeing the suffering of people left to the loan sharks, as this woman had been, and assuming that what they needed was charity. So we, as a nonprofit, would go in and build them a solution. And frankly, we'd done an imperfect and agonizingly slow job of it.

But this woman had shown me that she didn't need to wait for someone to come in and solve her water and sanitation problems for her. What she needed was someone to *invest* in her so she could solve these problems herself.

I'll tell you more about what I did with that realization in a moment. But first, there's something important you need to know about the water crisis, which the conversation in the slum that day threw into sharp relief: people living in poverty pay absurd prices for water. In fact, they typically pay far more than what middle-class people who are connected to water utilities pay. And that's true regardless of whether we're talking about cities or rural areas, about regions that are water rich or water poor.

In slums, most people get water delivered by tanker trucks. Think of it as a massive black market in water. Or, in some cases, a gray market—the tankers often have the blessing of local authorities, who see this as the only feasible way their communities are going to get water.

Either way, there's a lot of profit being made on the backs of the poor. The prices they're forced to shell out for tanker water are ten to fifteen times higher than what people pay when they're connected to water utilities and water flows from the tap. In Mumbai, water from trucks is *fifty-two times* more expensive.[3] I've met people who are spending 20 percent of their income on water. For an average American household living on an income of $60,000, that would be about $12,000 a year spent on water. Even stocking your fridge with Evian and drinking several gallons a day would cost less than that. For people in poverty, it's a crippling cost, but they have to spend it—their survival is at stake. One woman who gets her water delivered by tanker truck puts it like this: "Whatever it costs, we pay. We have no choice."[4]

In these same regions, families who don't have funding for a toilet sometimes pay out of pocket, multiple times a day, to use public latrines—spending far more on sanitation over the course of a lifetime than it would cost to simply install a toilet. Others avoid paying for public facilities by going to the bathroom out in the open—which, as I've mentioned, contaminates the very water they're paying high prices to drink. So people in these communities are forced to bear another cost: medical bills. In some slums, a hospital visit can cost nearly fifteen dollars—more than a week's wages when you live on two dollars a day.

It's expensive to be poor.

We call these expenses "coping costs"—the enormous amount of money lost every day, mostly by the poorest people on the planet, because they lack the funds to build a more sustainable solution.

If anything, the numbers above underestimate the costs, because coping costs are paid not only in money but in time. I actually wrote my graduate school thesis on this. I tried to tally the cost of labor that was being wasted—almost entirely by women, since they did the work—due to the lack of water and sanitation infrastructure. I brought a team of researchers to the slums around Tegucigalpa, Honduras. We each traveled to different public water taps and recorded the amount of time people spent walking to them, waiting for water, and walking home. Using local wage rates, we determined how much all of this wasted labor was actually worth. Then, by comparing the cost of installing a tap with the value of the labor each tap would save, we calculated how many taps the city should build. We found that the city should install so many taps that virtually every home would have one.

So people walk, stand, and wait all day—just to cope. They carry water for hours—to cope. They pay exorbitant rates for dirty water—to cope. They pay the resulting hospital bills—to cope. They pay ruinous interest rates to loan sharks—to cope. Every year, around the world, the amount of money people pour into these coping costs is *$300 billion.* When you realize that, the water crisis stops looking like a charity case. It starts looking, instead, like a market failure. There's money in the system—a lot of money in the system—but it's wasted, misallocated. Yet if those coping costs could be redirected—shifted somehow from short-term, stop-gap, dead-end solutions like dirty water from tanker trucks, and applied to permanent, cost-efficient solutions like water taps in homes—then people could do a lot more than cope. They could defy, and perhaps someday escape, the circumstances that had trapped them their entire lives.

I'd spent more than a decade working to convince Americans, mostly, to invest in ending the water crisis. But the people most willing and able to invest had been in front of me the whole time—on my trips to the field. I just hadn't seen it.

Suddenly the idea took shape, and the idea was simple. If people in poverty could manage to get a small, fair loan, they could use it to fund more permanent solutions. And then they could take some of what they'd been spending on coping costs and use it instead to pay back the loan.

Why loan the money? Why not just give it to them, as a gift, as a grant? A reasonable question, but I already knew the answer from years of raising money so we could provide more grants for projects: there's never enough. Once you give it away, it's gone for good; you're back at square one. But the thing about a loan is that it gets paid back. And as it does, that very same money can go right back out the door and help somebody else. And so on. In this way, a small loan could do a lot more good for a lot more people than a grant of the same size.

Once the idea occurred to me, it seemed almost obvious. For an engineer, that tends to be a good sign: in general, the simpler your design, the greater the chance it actually works. But it can also be a danger sign. After all, if the idea is so obvious, why isn't someone already doing it? It wasn't like the financial dynamics around water and sanitation were some big secret— my graduate studies at UNC focused at least as much on finance as engineering. Much of the research in my department was funded by the World Bank and concerned people's "willingness and ability to pay" for water and sanitation services. For academics, there was a sense that research and analysis could point to new, finance-led solutions to this crisis.

So the more I thought about it, the more I was convinced that this would work. But I wasn't shouting *Eureka!* just yet. Maybe there was a catch, something I was missing. I wanted to test this in the real world, tie it back to my academic training, and build the evidence base.

Our first attempt showed just how tough it could be to make

that work. One of our NGO partners in Kenya had binders overstuffed with requests for community water projects—far more than they could get funded in a reasonable time frame. So in 2003, we piloted a new approach: we lent capital to a few NGOs, which would in turn offer loans to these communities. The villages could keep waiting for the free well, which would likely take years or even decades, or they could build one immediately—if they paid the cost of construction back over time, once it started operating. It made sense in theory: since people in the community wouldn't have to keep paying coping costs once the project was finished, they could all pitch in to repay the loan, as the village would collect modest water tariffs once the water was flowing.

Several communities decided to take out a loan. What followed was a disaster—or actually a series of them. Things went awry from the start. In one village, the water system we were installing needed electricity to run—and the electrical line installation got delayed again and again. That was just one of many construction delays, which tend to happen a lot in developing countries. So the loans started to collect interest, and the communities weren't collecting the money they needed to make their payments—after all, they couldn't exactly charge people for water that wasn't flowing. Eventually, the communities put new people in charge of the water systems—people who felt no obligation to pay us back, since they hadn't made the loan agreement in the first place, and anyhow, why should they have to pay when we and our NGO partners had given water projects to *other* communities for free? And what options did we have when they refused to pay? Neither we nor our partners had much legal recourse to enforce these agreements in Kenya.

At the end of the day, we were paid back about fifty cents on the dollar. We learned that lending—especially in extremely poor places—is really tough business. You need for people to think of you as an entity that *needs* to be repaid, which was always going to be tough for an NGO. And you have to have the enormous expertise required to evaluate risk, to allow for it, to take every step you can to mitigate it. Neither Water-Partners nor our partner NGOs had that expertise.

At the WaterPartners offices we soon had a new mantra: *You can't turn an NGO into a bank.*

We'd found the catch.

Of course, failing never feels great. But this time, it also felt like progress. You can't solve the problem standing in the way of your idea until you find it. We'd figured out that we didn't know how to sustainably lend money in these places. So the next logical question was: Who *does*?

There's a great story behind the answer to that question—so let me take you for a moment to a village in southern Bangladesh in 1976. A young economics professor was visiting the community to conduct research. His name was Muhammad Yunus. You might have heard of him—years later, he won the Nobel Peace Prize for the work he began in the village that day.

After watching a famine devastate the country several years earlier, Yunus had decided to focus on poverty reduction, so he was in the village to speak with the community's poorest residents. He started a conversation with a woman named Sufiya, who made bamboo furniture for a living. She told him that she never had enough money for raw materials, so a local trader was lending her the bamboo in exchange for her selling the furniture back to him. The trader made sure to pay her just enough to survive—but not so much that she could start saving money to buy the bamboo herself. Yunus saw Sufiya's situation as akin to slavery—all because no one would make her a fair loan that would allow her to buy the bamboo and break the cycle of dependence on this trade. Yunus heard many stories like this during his visit, so he asked one of his research assistants to find out who in the village was in a similar situation and how big a loan they'd need to break free of it.

A week later, she brought him a list of forty-two people. They needed the equivalent of twenty-seven dollars. Not per person—the entire group. "My God, my God," he said. "All this misery in all these families all for the lack of twenty-seven dollars!" He handed his research assistant the money and told her to lend it to the people in need, asking them to repay him whenever they could. He charged no interest.[5] Yunus had forty-two borrowers. Every one of them paid him back within a year.[6]

Of course, he didn't have the funds to do this on a large scale. So he went to the local bank and asked if they could start making these "microloans." The banker nearly laughed him out of the room. Poor villagers couldn't even sign their names, the banker said, and they had no collateral—how could the bank possibly issue them a loan?[7] So Yunus went to a higher-up and negotiated a solution: if Yunus served as a guarantor, the bank would make the loans. For the next year, the professor personally signed every loan request that came from the villagers. Muhammad Yunus was on to something.

Yunus expanded his informal operation to two villages, then ten, then a hundred, until he decided to set up his own bank. After two years of tense negotiations with the Bangladeshi government and the central bank, which shared the bankers' conviction that people living in extreme poverty could never pay back loans, Yunus was granted permission to establish Grameen Bank. At the bank, he came up with new techniques to mitigate the risk of loaning to people in poverty. Grameen split up their loans into smaller, more frequent payments, for example; it helped set up groups of loan recipients who could provide one another with advice and support; and it sent bank representatives out into the community every week to answer questions and collect payments.[8]

These strategies worked. Within twenty years, Grameen Bank had expanded to 40,000 villages in Bangladesh and given loans to 2.4 million borrowers—95 percent of them women. For many of these women, the act of taking out a loan was itself empowering. As Professors Rohini Pande and Erica Field point out, a woman in poverty might find that it is "perhaps the first time she engages with the world outside the domestic sphere and, importantly, with other women."[9] And the effects can be transformative. In a country where children from poor families often don't get an education, nearly every child of every Grameen client was attending school. In Bangladesh's 1997 municipal elections, more than 2,000 Grameen members were elected to local government offices.[10]

It's an incredible story. If you can't tell by now, Muhammad Yunus is one of my heroes. He's a hero, in fact, to a lot of people around the world—to people whose lives he has helped transform, and to organizations that, in one way or another, are applying his model of microfinance to solve different kinds of problems. After Grameen Bank's success, many organizations followed its lead. I'd seen microfinance growing firsthand during my time at Catholic Relief Services. By the time of my conversation with the woman in the Indian slum in 2003, there were over a hundred million microfinance borrowers in the world. The industry was especially strong where it had begun, in Bangladesh, as well as neighboring India.

Coincidentally, microfinance was really taking off around the time WaterPartners started looking for local lending partners. The UN declared 2005 the International Year of Microfinance. From 2004 to 2006, the global microfinance market doubled in size.[11]

In 2006, when Yunus won the Nobel Peace Prize, the announcement read: "Loans to poor people without any financial security had appeared to be an impossible idea. From modest beginnings three decades ago, Yunus has, first and foremost through Grameen Bank, developed micro-credit into an ever more important instrument in the struggle against poverty."

In a lot of ways, microfinance institutions—or MFIs, as we started saying, once we were talking about them too often to use all eight syllables—seemed like perfect partners for us. They were concentrated in areas where the water crisis was raging, and they knew how to lend sustainably in challenging environments. And while our skill sets were different, our goals were the same: like us, MFIs valued social good over profit.

So again, I kept thinking: there's no reason why water and sanitation loans shouldn't work.

I quickly found that there were two big barriers standing in the way.

The first barrier was that MFIs didn't loan money to entire communities—they loaned money to individuals or small groups. And that was key to their strategy: MFIs knew that microloans work only when people feel an acute sense of responsibility and ownership over a loan, which is more likely to happen when the borrower is an individual. (Lending to institutions works, too, but they need to be strong, well-managed entities that can identify and manage various forms of risk.) In other words, borrowers are more likely to feel a meaningful obligation to repay when that obligation isn't diffused across hundreds of people.

WaterPartners, however, had always provided water and sanitation solutions that worked for entire communities, not individual households. It was counterintuitive that the best way to reach more people, more efficiently, would be to pursue solutions that served *fewer* people. Yet we'd learned when we issued our first loan in Kenya that the MFIs were right: it didn't work to provide loans to weak local institutions that lacked accountability and incentives to repay. And we soon realized that there was a lot individual households could do with a microloan—typically fifty to five hundred dollars—to solve their water and sanitation problems.[12]

In slums, water and sewage pipes often run underneath the feet of people who simply aren't connected to them. With a microloan, they can pay the connection fee and get taps and toilets connected to the city's system. In more rural areas not yet covered by utilities, people can install a rainwater collection system or drill a small family well to get their water. For sanitation, they can build a pit toilet and septic tank, where sewage begins to safely decompose underground and then gets emptied periodically for further treatment. All were meaningful solutions that microloans could fund. I was convinced that households would want to take out these loans—if I could just convince MFIs to offer them.

◊

There was one more barrier, however, standing in the way of my idea. And this one proved far more difficult to surmount.

I started cold-calling MFIs to see if they'd be interested in working with us to issue water and sanitation loans. To be clear, I wasn't just picking up an Indian phone book and calling MFIs at random. I focused on MFIs that were recommended to me by the people I'd met who had taken out microloans to kick-start their businesses of one kind or another: businesses that made clothing or crafts, for example. So these MFIs came approved by the loan recipients themselves—an important endorsement. I put together a list and started making calls. Then I learned why they call them "cold" calls. The first MFI that I reached wasn't interested. Neither was the second. Or the third, or the fourth. You get the picture.

I think a lot of people would have gotten the message by then and stopped calling. But I am that dog with a bone. It is difficult for me to leave a challenge, or even a discussion, without exhausting all the reasons why or what-ifs—just ask my wife and kids! When I tore my meniscus about a decade ago, my doctor told me in no uncertain terms that I needed surgery, and even if I got it, I'd never run again. Because of all my international travel, I had to delay the surgery. I started to wonder if there was another way. About this time, I realized how out of shape I'd gotten—my body mass index indicated I was overweight. So I shed some pounds, did some strengthening, and on a whim one day, I tried running again. When that felt okay, I started running a little more. Eventually, I decided to train for a marathon. I've now completed two—and never wound up getting that surgery.

So suffice it to say I wasn't going to let a couple of "no"s get me down. I kept emailing. Sometimes I just showed up at the door of the MFI. I did this for a year—reaching MFI after MFI, not one of them willing to lend money for water and sanitation projects. At least they did me the courtesy of telling me why: because water and sanitation loans didn't directly generate income. This is what they told me again and again. When I got the chance to talk with Muhammad Yunus about this, even he was discouraging. He told me that the MFIs were right, that water and sanitation microloans were never going to be a large-scale solution. MFIs in the early 2000s saw microloans as investments in small businesses, not in improving living conditions. Asking an MFI to make a water and sanitation loan was a little like asking a venture capitalist to finance your mortgage. It's just not their line of work.

Now, to be fair, there's a good reason the MFIs saw things that way. As Yunus himself learned when he was first launching microfinance, people in poverty don't have collateral to guarantee a loan. Nor do they have credit scores that help a bank know how likely they are to repay it. MFIs in the developing world just didn't have the tools or the data to determine who can afford a loan and who can't. Instead, they listened carefully to how a person intended to use the loan. For example, a loan officer might meet with a woman who asks for fifty dollars so she can buy a sewing machine, which she'll use to make clothes she can sell. She explains that she can sell each skirt for a net profit of a dollar, and she can make three skirts every day. In that way, a fifty-dollar investment can yield ninety dollars in profit each month. That makes her a pretty good bet for the bank; she'll very likely be able to repay the loan.

But if the same woman asks for a loan to build a toilet in her home—how's she going to pay that back? MFIs didn't know enough about the market dynamics behind water and sanitation to answer this question, and they weren't all that interested in learning more about it. If anything, they were getting even more stringent in requiring that their microloans generated income. In the mid-2000s, the boom in microfinance was creating a backlash about overindebtedness: there was a stream of stories about people having to sell their houses or pawn their food ration cards in order to repay their loans.[13] There were reports of loan officers verbally and physically harassing borrowers, seizing their valuables, and staging sit-ins outside their homes to publicly shame them.[14] In 2010, the government in one Indian state, Andhra Pradesh, shut down the area's microfinance industry, noting that over the course of just a few months, more than eighty people who'd defaulted on microloans took their own lives.[15]

Clearly, in some places, the microfinance sector had grown too fast and bank officials had gone too far, providing loans indiscriminately and then, in effect, blaming the victims—the recipients. It took some time for the system, with a nudge from the Indian government's central bank, to rid itself of bad actors. But even the good actors had been chastened by the experience and resolved to be more careful than ever about the loans they issued, and to whom, and for what.

Muhammad Yunus once said, famously, "All human beings are born entrepreneurs."[16] But the more I thought about that statement, the more I came to disagree with its premise: that with a little startup capital, just about anybody could start a business and take a first step on the path to self-sufficiency. After all, the lack of startup capital is only one of many things keeping people in poverty. Consider, again, any one of the millions of women who spend their days fetching water. She has no time to start a business. Or consider any one of the millions of people afflicted by waterborne diseases. They're too sick to start a business.

When you look at it that way, it becomes clear why, over time, studies revealed that microfinance wasn't nearly as powerful a tool for breaking the cycle of poverty as development economists had once hoped. Certain human needs—fundamental needs— have to be served before a person can even make use of an enterprise loan. MFIs, for the reasons I've mentioned, didn't see any role for themselves in helping people meet those basic needs. But something interesting was going on, right under the lenders' noses. For years, their clients had been quietly using their loans to invest in whatever they needed most urgently: school fees, medical treatment, home repairs, and other nonbusiness purposes. In many cases this meant breaking the terms of the loan. During the backlash against microfinance, new studies revealed the extent of the practice—among them a 2008 study showing that in Indonesia more than half of poor households that had taken microloans ended up using them for nonbusiness purposes.[17]

At first, this was seen as a failure, an indictment of microfinance. But what if this was actually one of its most important

features? In some cases, people were using these loans to relieve their most immediate suffering—to buy medicine for a
sick child or put food on the table. Countless nonprofits spend
countless dollars trying to meet these same needs less effectively. Also, using loans this way revealed how narrow the
MFIs' definition of "income generating" had been. When someone gets treatment for a sickness *before* it turns into a lifelong
disability, there's no doubt that they're enhancing their ability
to earn an income (and therefore pay their loan back). And—as
we at WaterPartners had been insisting—when someone has a
water tap installed in her home and no longer has to spend four
hours a day collecting water, she's just opened up half her day
for paid work. Maybe it wasn't *directly* income generating. But
indirectly, and indisputably, it was setting in motion a virtuous
cycle of opportunity.

If MFIs could give people the freedom to invest in meeting their most urgent needs without tempting them into over-
borrowing, that might be the biggest contribution microfinance
had made yet.

I might not have had the confidence to keep pushing this message if not for a conference in Monterey, California, that I'd
been attending since before it was a household name: TED.

I've heard it said that an engineering degree is about teaching you how to think. It was my "TED matriculation," however, that truly taught me how to think differently, expansively.

TED is all about cultivating curiosity and finding new ways to look at challenges. At other conferences, I felt like I was surrounded by people who were a lot like me. I'm always happy to be among other engineers, but at TED, the point was to bring together ideas that seemed, on the surface, to have nothing to do with your day job. It was great training in how to harness disparate concepts to create something new.

At TED, I met Steven Johnson, who wrote a great book titled *Where Good Ideas Come From*. What I took away from the book is that there is no such thing as a truly original idea, that every good idea has its roots in someone else's good idea. I started to understand that what we'd done at WaterPartners—borrowing Yunus's concepts and blending them with the market realities of water and sanitation—fit a well-established pattern for game-changing ideas.

TED also taught me that it's one thing to latch on to a good idea, but it's quite another to get other people to believe in it. That requires a totally different skill set. I started to accept that it was incumbent on me to make people believe—to figure out how to use my passion and tenacity to share what TED calls an "idea worth spreading."

And so I kept at it—until finally, after a year of searching, I found an organization that saw things as we did. It was called BASIX, and it was based in Hyderabad, the Indian city where I had the conversation in the slum that set this whole idea in motion. BASIX had conducted a study about how their microloans were changing people's lives through entrepreneurship—and had been disappointed, even perplexed, by the results. Only half the people who'd been with the bank for at least three years had seen their incomes increase—and not by much, about 10 percent on average. One in four clients said nothing had changed. And worst of all, about the same number had fallen deeper into poverty. BASIX came to the same realization I had: the barriers to rising out of poverty were complicated, and traditional business microloans weren't addressing all of them.[18]

The founder of BASIX, Vijay Mahajan, explains that this ignited a big debate in the organization. They could keep going down what he called the "orthodox microfinance road"—giving simple business startup loans—or try to develop a new service that better addressed people's complicated needs. The latter choice, as Vijay put it, was "more complex, messier, and infinitely harder to manage and control" than the traditional path, but it "had a chance (whether 50/50, 20/80, or 90/10, no one could say) of making much more of a difference."[19] So BASIX chose the second path, and began by offering more loan options—going beyond loans that people would need to grow a business.

They had just started this process when we approached them about water and sanitation loans. After I explained what people were paying in coping costs, Vijay and his team began to see why people should be able to repay these loans—even though they didn't directly generate income. So after a year of hearing no, we finally got a yes.

It was a qualified yes. BASIX wasn't ready to include water and sanitation loans in their regular portfolio, because if the loans went unpaid, they would drag down the bank's reputation and creditworthiness. So BASIX decided to call it research and development and tuck it into a separate unit—in effect, to put a fence around it until it proved itself. At long last, we had a partner willing to take a measured risk.

And I do mean measured. In order for BASIX to launch the pilot program, WaterPartners would need to pay for it. We were essentially paying to derisk this new program for BASIX so they could see some evidence that it worked before they risked their own capital. We were fine with that—because where they saw doubt and risk, we saw near certainty of success.

We had an understanding with BASIX that if the pilot was successful, the bank would take this type of loan mainstream and scale it up. We were in business.

◊

It took several years, but eventually the results of the pilot began to come in. I'd been making the case for a long time that families would be able to pay back these loans. But all along I'd had to acknowledge that this was a theory. Until now, we hadn't had the opportunity to test it in the real world. Now we were doing just that, and it was one of the most gratifying experiences of my life.

We ran the numbers. And here we had it, the percentage of people who paid back the loans, in full and on time: 97 percent.

The numbers were staggering—they were thrilling. The stories behind them, even more so. Our clients were women like Leneriza, whom I got a chance to meet in the Philippines.

I've mentioned that I met people who spent a fifth of their income on water. Well, Leneriza was one of them.[20] She told me she'd been buying water from a local vendor for sixty dollars a month. But then, with her loan, she was able to get a water tap installed in her house. She made her loan payments and paid her new water utility bill happily—because together they added up to less than ten dollars a month. She had clean, safe water *and* fifty dollars a month more to support her family.

The reality, it turned out, was even better than the theory.

With evidence like this now in hand, it got easier to make our case to MFIs. Suresh Krishna, the leader of one of the most innovative MFIs in India (today called CreditAccess Grameen), not only agreed to start a water and sanitation loan program, but also offered to use the MFI's own capital for the loans. Soon, more MFIs started signing on—and, even better, started including water and sanitation loan programs in their core business, instead of some R&D offshoot.

We also continued with our more traditional model of subsidized community-based water projects. But the limits of these projects were becoming more apparent now that we were seeing what loans could do. Providing a grant to cover the cost of a new water system was a one and done project. It couldn't be scaled: once you used the money you'd raised, you were back on the road to raise money for the next project. Microloans don't work like that: in time, they can become essentially self-generating, as repayments serve as sources of future loans for other borrowers. Because of this, they require only a slight nudge from us before they gain their own momentum—allowing their impact to build on itself.

This, I could see, was a solution that could scale. So quickly the question in my mind began to change from *Could this possibly work?* to *How big could this possibly get?*

In 2008, the Gates Foundation researched the demand for water and sanitation microloans. They put the number at $12 billion.[21] That sounds small to me now—because today, we know the number is actually far bigger. But at the time, it sounded enormous—earthshaking.

Up to that point, WaterPartners had been trying to help solve a several-hundred-billion-dollar problem with resources that—even after over a decade of work—still only measured in the millions. So it was no wonder that progress always seemed so slow—why we always seemed to be inching toward a goal we could barely see, a goal that never seemed to get closer.

But if we could get $12 *billion* invested in solving the crisis, we wouldn't just be slogging along anymore. We'd be sprinting.

4

THE MEET-CUTE

POV: Matt Damon

The biggest turning point in my work on water came in 2008, when I went to the annual meeting of the Clinton Global Initiative.

The mission of CGI is "to turn ideas into action," which at first glance probably strikes you as so generic that it could describe just about any organization. (Are there any organizations whose mission is to "turn ideas into inaction," or "to make sure ideas never get beyond the idea stage"?) But when Bill Clinton came up with the concept in 2005, it had at least a little bit of edge. After attending the World Economic Forum in Davos, Clinton issued a complaint I'm sure you've heard before, from others: that elites were getting together at that upscale ski resort, talking big about making the world a better place, and then returning to business as usual. "I just see all these people leave here every year full of energy," Clinton said, "wanting to *do something* and wanting to know there is a place where they can actually go and say, Okay, what is my assignment?" At CGI, he said, participants were not just going to be asked to express their opinions about issues, but to "make very specific commitments" to address them, and then, the next year, to be graded publicly on their progress. "We need to know, we did *this thing* and it got *that result*," he said.[1]

Clinton and his team planned the conference to coincide with the huge influx of heads of state and other VIPs that come to New York every September for the UN General Assembly. The city is always immobilized that week, gridlocked by motorcades, but Clinton had no trouble filling the New York Sheraton with participants: more than fifty current or former heads of state; well over a hundred CEOs; presidents of global foundations; and, of course, Bono. Also legendary athletes-turned-activists like Muhammad Ali. Also me: an actor who once did the voice for a cartoon horse in a movie called *Spirit: Stallion of the Cimarron*. (Fortunately, I don't think anybody in this crowd had seen it.)[2]

I remember that the meeting kicked off with a keynote by Gordon Brown, then the prime minister of Great Britain. Clinton introduced him as a man who knew as much about the world as anybody he'd ever met—and it was as if Brown took it as a challenge. He spoke for nearly an hour without notes, moving deftly from topic to topic, delivering insights about the policy changes that could make life better for people in poverty. It was an impressive performance. But, then, I felt that way about so many of the speeches I heard at the conference, and not just the headliners. The speaker who followed Brown was a doctor who had spent his life studying tropical diseases—diseases that get a small fraction of the attention and funding they need because they're virtually unheard of in wealthy countries like the United States. "Usually when I talk about my job," he said, "it's to three or four people." He gestured to President Clinton: "It's a testament to you that we've filled a room to talk about parasitic worms."[3]

And really, it was. Clinton beamed with pride. This is what he loves doing: using his magnetic pull to draw all kinds of people into the same room, people who might not have ever met otherwise, and who now, thanks to him, might find a way to do big, or bigger, things together. The whole conference was engineered with that in mind. The panels were set up that way. The gala dinner looked like a big party, and was, but it was planned with military precision. Everything was about results, outcomes, partnerships, plans. The Sheraton was ringed with what the organizers called "whisper rooms"—which I recognize makes it sound like a very different kind of conference, but you'll have to trust me when I tell you that the whispering was about things like global financing facilities. There was nothing sexy about it (unless you're into that sort of thing, in which case you came to the right conference).

All in all, there was a lot of talking going on, but as I made my way from keynote address to panel discussion to breakout session, it seemed to me that Clinton was succeeding in his goal: the whole event was oriented toward action. And not just action, but accountability. When participants pledged to do something, the commitments were announced publicly, which created a kind of social pressure for others to step up, too. (In 2008 alone, the commitments added up to $8 billion.)[4] And the results were announced publicly, too—so if you missed your target, then at the next CGI, all your fancy powerful friends were going to know about it.

The Economist covered the conference, and the reporter, I think, had it about right: "Mr. Brown reminded us that when Cicero spoke, people said, 'That was a good speech.' When Demosthenes spoke, people marched. They are marching, here at the Sheraton New York."[5] I had my boots on, too, but I still wasn't sure where exactly I was heading.

When I met Gary White, the thing that impressed me most about him was that he kept telling me about all the times he'd failed.

The two of us had been set up in one of those whisper rooms at CGI after a few of my H_2O Africa partners met Gary and realized he could help us get a lot smarter about our work. Well, we had been promised a whisper room, but where the CGI staff actually parked us was in a massive, and empty, hotel ballroom, like an airplane hangar with chandeliers. I was standing at one end of the room in total quiet, thinking— as one might in such circumstances—*This is weird.*

And getting weirder. When Gary came in, he entered the ballroom on the opposite side, which meant we had to take a long, awkward walk to reach each other, grinning uncomfortably all the way. It had all the absurd drama of the meet-cute scenes you see in rom-coms, and I felt like I needed to break the tension. "Hey!" I shouted. "Let's talk water."

We sat down and introduced ourselves, and I started asking him about his work. At events like CGI, people often give in to the temptation to inflate their own accomplishments. And my H_2O Africa partners had told me enough about Gary that I knew he had plenty of accomplishments to inflate. But he didn't inflate them. If anything, he did the opposite. He told me about his work at Catholic Relief Services—and where it fell short. He explained that he had come up with a new approach to water projects, an approach that worked brilliantly—on a small scale. He was quick to say he had been unable to build it up enough to make a dent in the crisis. He described another idea he'd had, one he thought had the potential to change everything—the idea was to give small water and sanitation loans to people in poverty—but said that the first time he tried it in Kenya, it failed.

As sales pitches go, this was as restrained as they get. It was almost an anti-sales pitch. If CGI was the speed-dating service of the development world, my potential match here was opening with all his flaws, his greatest mistakes, his personal failings. And it was working for me. On a personal level, I was drawn to Gary's modesty. But what really struck me as I sat there talking with him, what really impressed me the most, was his comfort level with failure—his willingness to accept it as an inevitable, and indispensable, part of the process. Not something to be spun or explained away, not something to be avoided at all costs, but something that informs your approach and fuels your success.

Now, I know the importance of failure is one of those counterintuitive lessons that's become so cliché that it's no longer counterintuitive. It's a staple of the commencement addresses that graduates hear every spring, right up there with "follow your dreams" in the running for Most Obvious Advice Ever. I've offered that advice myself. I was lucky to have success in my profession at a young age, in my twenties, but not until I'd had a taste of what it's like to fail, what it's like to hit a wall, repeatedly, often with your head. Ben Affleck and I spent our first decade as actors doing something we called being "OK thanksed." Being "OK thanksed" entailed getting on a bus from Boston to New York for an audition, waiting our turn among all the other guys who looked just like us, crying our eyes out for a casting director in what we thought was a real Oscar moment, then being told "OK, thanks." That was it. No praise, no pat on the head, not even any constructive criticism, just a disinvested "OK, thanks." Hearing it always hurt. Eventually we were able to see it as part of the process—to accept that we were going to have to log a bunch of "no"s before we were going to get a "yes."

When I started my water work I expected I was going to have to go through something similar, and I did. In this case

I didn't take it personally. Even early on, I'd learned enough about water and sanitation to know just how ineffective most water projects were—and I had no interest in doing this work poorly. I anticipated—correctly, it turned out—that as H_2O Africa tried to craft a better strategy, we'd make grants that turned out to be a bad bet, we'd support projects that sputtered and went nowhere, and we'd bet on exciting new ideas that went up in smoke. I accepted all this as the price of admission to a world in which I was not nearly an expert, but where I thought I had something to contribute.

But Gary, who very clearly was an expert, was much further along in this process than I was. The fact that he'd spent twenty years logging plenty of "no"s told me that he'd been bold enough to keep trying new ideas—facing failures forthrightly, learning lessons, finding success. And that meant he was avoiding that much bigger, far more concerning failure: incremental solutions that did not add up, and would never add up, to the ultimate goal of providing water and sanitation access for everyone. Gary was billed as a water and sanitation engineer, but to me, he looked like an innovator—and exactly the kind of partner I'd been looking for. As we talked, an hour passed before I knew it, and suddenly I realized I was almost late for a meeting with President Clinton. Which would be really bad form. I invited Gary to come along with me, and together we made our way through the Sheraton to track down the president. My speed-date with Gary had been a success, and Clinton, our match-maker, would be the first to know about it.

The more I learned about WaterPartners, the more confident I became that they were implementing water projects better than anyone. I was struck by the way Gary spoke about the communities they worked with, not just as recipients of water projects, but as leaders in designing, constructing, and running these projects. WaterPartners' success rate showed that this approach worked over the long term. Based on everything I'd heard from Gary and others, and based, if I'm honest, just on the feeling I had in talking with Gary, I was ready to entrust WaterPartners with a good portion of the money we'd been raising through H_2O Africa.

But of course the thing that had Gary most excited wasn't drilling wells. It was his new idea, WaterCredit. At that point, WaterCredit's pilot programs in India were seeing promising results, and there was the potential for much greater success ahead: at CGI, the commitment Gary was announcing was a $4 million grant from the PepsiCo Foundation to start testing WaterCredit on a larger scale.[6] This was big news, and not just because of the dollar sign attached. The PepsiCo grant was an encouraging sign that global corporations—some of them at least—could be persuaded to get engaged in addressing the water crisis. The company's CEO, Indra Nooyi, had made clear that she understood just how essential a clean, plentiful supply of water was to the beverages they made, and she was determined to make a difference on the issue writ large, not just as it pertained to Pepsi plants. As she put it: "Water is an integral part of PepsiCo's business ecosystem, and ensuring access to clean, reliable sources of water is vital to the health and livelihood of communities around the world."[7] So she was making a $4 million bet on Gary's particular approach to the problem.

To be honest, at first I had a hard time fully accepting the idea behind WaterCredit. It felt strange to me, or maybe worse than strange, to think of charging extremely poor people for something they need in order to survive. Imagine coming across someone in a desert who is dying of thirst, and instead of giving them your water bottle, asking them if they want to buy it from you. It felt, when I first heard it described, like the parts of capitalism that make a lot of us uneasy. It just felt wrong. It felt wrong to ask some of the poorest people on the planet to take what little they had and to spend it on something—water—that we in rich nations often get for free, or almost free. Putting it generously: it's not intuitive.

At least it wasn't until I heard Gary out. As we talked, he got me to face some facts. If we wanted to solve the crisis, the world needed to increase its spending on water and sanitation development by about $100 billion every year for the next ten years.[8, 9] That kind of funding gap wasn't going to be closed by me asking for donations in TV ads with Sarah McLachlan playing in the background. (Actually, Gary was too polite to say that part, but I know he was thinking it.) Realistically, the gap wasn't going to be closed even if governments around the world decided to make water and sanitation a higher priority. Even declaring another Water Decade would not get it done. Those were the facts I had to confront. The message of the numbers Gary rattled off was not "let's try harder." It was "we need a paradigm shift."

But—and this was the exciting part—he was able to describe what that new paradigm could be. As he explained, there were hundreds of millions of people around the world who, despite their very low incomes, were able to pay a reasonable price for water and sanitation, and who, incredibly, were eager to pay for a reliable source of water and sanitation—if only they were given the chance. By insisting that charity was the only moral, workable way to help, we were, it seemed, limiting our options, limiting our ambitions, and perpetuating the problem. Worse yet, we were underestimating the resourcefulness of the very people we wanted to help.

As our conversation continued, I started to look at the water crisis differently. I started to see it, at its core, as a finance problem. In order to understand why that is, you have to understand what people are actually paying for when they pay for water and sanitation.

In an excellent book called *The Big Thirst*, journalist Charles Fishman describes a little sign that a hotel chain once put on the bottles of water in its guest rooms. "It's water," the sign read. "Of course it's free."[10] As Fishman notes, the sign lays bare a contradiction in our thinking. On the one hand, *of course* water is free: it literally falls from the sky. Yet at the same time, *of course* water costs something: that's why you get a utility bill every month. So which is it?

As Gary explained, water utilities aren't really charging us for the water.[11] The bill we pay is for the cost of water *delivery*. We're paying for someone to go get the water from wherever it naturally is in the water cycle at a given moment (in a lake, in pools of rainwater, underground), clean the water, and deliver it through the pipes to our taps, or to a store in bottles.

The same is true of sanitation—in the opposite direction. Of course, what comes out of our bodies, to borrow an appropriate saying, isn't worth shit. But we pay every month, often as part of that same water utility bill, for sewage to be taken *away* from the places we live and eat.

So when you pay for water and sanitation, what you're paying is essentially a shipping fee.

Of course, these days, Amazon has many of us thinking that shipping is free, too. But water and sanitation create some of the biggest delivery challenges in the world. Sewage is produced every day by every human on the planet. And if this isn't obvious, sewage is toxic waste—waste that can spread deadly disease if you don't immediately transport it away from where you live.

As for water, it is far and away the heaviest substance we rely on to survive. Imagine a camping trip: you can pretty easily carry on your back all the food, shelter, and warm clothing you need in order to spend a few days in the woods. It's water that presents a problem. The minimum amount of water a family of four needs each day for basic drinking, cooking, and washing weighs *sixty-six pounds*.[12] Nothing else that we require in order to survive weighs anything close to that. And we need it constantly—every time we drink or eat or clean or bathe or go to the bathroom. In other words, water and sanitation delivery on the scale the world needs would confound even Amazon. (Ironic, since Amazon is named after one of the biggest water delivery systems in the world.)

For millennia, humans have solved this problem by building systems that do this for us. We build grand infrastructure for our cities—reservoirs, dams, sewer pipes, canals. And in more remote villages or households, we build smaller-scale infrastructure—wells, septic tanks, irrigation ditches, rainwater collection systems.

If you add up the cost of all the human labor it takes to transport water and sewage by hand, you see that it costs much more in the long run. As Gary explained, the coping costs are high. But building the infrastructure to avoid these costs requires large sums of money up front—and large sums are, by definition, what people living in poverty don't have. So they're stuck moving water and sewage in far less efficient—and far costlier— ways than we have in the developed world.

So, at its core, the problem with building water and sanitation infrastructure isn't exactly that it's too expensive, because the coping costs it eliminates save money over the long term. The problem is that it requires so much capital up front. Like I said—a finance problem.

Yet there couldn't have been a worse time than September 2008 for Gary to be pitching finance as a solution to one of the world's biggest problems. At that moment, the financial industry *was* one of the world's biggest problems.

A week before I went to CGI, I was on a flight that stopped for a layover. As we all sat on the runway checking our phones, an investment banker on the plane started to panic. Lehman Brothers had just collapsed. He said: "A nuclear bomb just went off in the global economy." It was, of course, only a slight overstatement. The financial crisis that followed would become the worst the world had faced since the Great Depression, and for a while it looked like the sequel might be bigger than the original.

By the time Gary and I met at CGI, US lawmakers had drafted a $700 billion bank bailout bill to prevent further financial institutions from collapsing. Over a thousand protesters stood outside the New York Stock Exchange carrying signs that called the bailout a CLASS WAR CRIME—while a couple of subway stops away, we were rubbing elbows with the people who'd be executing the bailout *and* the people who created the need for it.[13] Even the CEO of Lehman Brothers was scheduled to come.[14] He canceled.

Despite the company I was keeping at that moment, I agreed with the protesters. Not long after that, I narrated a documentary, *Inside Job*, which showed how lenders had exploited vulnerable Americans, luring them into mortgage loans they couldn't afford, only to have taxpayers foot the bill when the scheme came crashing down. It was one more reason to be skeptical of a plan to give loans to people who were already struggling financially.

◊

At the same time, there was a world of difference between the big banks that were tanking the global economy and the microlenders that were giving borrowers the chance to break the cycle of poverty and take control of their own lives.

I'd had a memorable introduction to microfinance when I visited Zambia in 2006. We'd gone to a remote village and stopped at a market set up by entrepreneurs whose business ideas had been funded with microloans. There were farmers selling produce they'd grown, tailors selling clothes they'd made, food vendors selling meals they'd cooked. Then, in between two mud brick stalls, a man had shoved rows of plastic chairs and set up a curtain to block out the light. And in this small, almost dark space, he'd placed a tiny TV with a VCR: a movie theater! Brilliant. This guy was speaking my language. He was charging people something like ten cents to get in. I wondered what was playing—what he had running for today's matinee. I took a look at one of the bootleg DVDs he had on display. And there, looking back at me from the cover of this DVD case, in the middle of Zambia, was my own face. Today's feature was *The Bourne Supremacy*. I guess I'm not supposed to condone, you know, piracy, but we all just started laughing. We took a bunch of pictures with the guy, but we didn't stay for the movie. I already knew how it ended.

This stop was part of my education, engineered by ONE, and we talked a lot on that trip about the philosophy of Muhammad Yunus. I knew that for Yunus the goal was not for lenders to maximize profit, but to improve as many lives as possible in a sustainable way. The lenders have to benefit enough to have an incentive—and the means—to keep lending, but the emphasis is on the outcome, on what their loans enable their customers to do to improve their own lives. Of course, there are unscrupulous microlenders out there; but the weight of the evidence, over four decades, made clear that far more people had been empowered by microfinance than exploited by it. And WaterCredit seemed incredibly empowering. Once I learned that people's loan payments were less than the costs they'd incurred for stopgap solutions, I started to think that there might actually be such a thing as a market-based solution to the water and sanitation crisis.

Again, at the very moment that the financial sector had thrown the global economy into a ditch, the idea of enlisting the market in our efforts seemed, well, counterintuitive. What would Yunus say? Fortunately, we didn't have to guess. Yunus was there at CGI. Amid all the anxious and even angry talk about capitalism, Yunus was singing a different tune. In an interview, he said, "We have to get out of the mindset that the rich will do the business and the poor will have the charity."[15] He made a passionate case that finance—public enemy number one in 2008—could play an indispensable role in helping millions of people lift themselves out of poverty. He rejected, forcefully, the idea that the best hope for changing the circumstances of the world's poorest people was our generosity, rather than their resourcefulness.

I thought of my mother and how she had always warned me never to condescend to the people I was trying to help. She still thought charity was essential, and I did, too; I don't think any sensible person would argue otherwise. But one of the things that appealed to me about microfinance was that it started from the premise that people, whatever their economic circumstances, were capable of investing in their own solutions, of deciding what those solutions would be and how they would be applied. It started from a place of respect—the opposite of condescension, the opposite of arrogance.

I saw just how important that was a few months later, on a trip to Ethiopia. Our group came upon a well that probably cost about $10,000 to drill, lying in disrepair. Without the ability to fix it, the people in the community had gone to great effort to hand dig a well right next to it. When we visited, there were kids at that hand-dug well, drinking water that looked like chocolate milk. If my daughters were ever about to drink something like that, I'd dive over and knock it out of their hands. But that wouldn't do any good here—these kids were drinking it because it was the best option they had. The donated pump was offering only irony.

Compare that with the WaterCredit customers Gary had met when he visited the WaterCredit pilot programs. They'd show him the new water taps and toilets that they had chosen to meet their needs, that they'd worked hard for, that they had every interest in maintaining and even upgrading. He'd often see people proudly holding up the loan cards that had been marked each time they made a payment.

I realized: having the ability to assert control over your own life—to decide the future you want and work to make it a reality—is as universal a need as water.

The conversation that Gary and I started in that cavernous whisper room at CGI was the start of a rolling conversation that never really stopped (and still hasn't). Over the following months, as we wrapped our minds around the idea of working together—what that would mean, how that would work—I came back to Gary again and again with questions. A lot of them, if I'm honest, were pretty dumb. I kind of knew they were dumb, and Gary *definitely* knew they were dumb. But he answered every one with kindness and patience and, it was clear, wisdom. In fact, Gary's answers were so good that my brother, Kyle, and I both started going to him instinctively with unrelated questions, big, random questions about life, marriage, the universe—prompting Gary more than once to remind us: "Water, guys. Water. That's what I know about!"

The more we talked, the more confidence I had in Water-Credit. But I also believed that if WaterCredit didn't fulfill our hopes, if it hit an obstacle we didn't foresee, it would become one of those failures we learned from in later years. Of course we would hit a barrier somewhere along the way, but Gary was clearly a guy who would get back up and run straight at the next one. He was too committed to the work he was doing to just throw up his hands and say *Enough!* He had that essential blend of boldness, which you need in order to insist there's a smarter way to solve a problem, and humility, which you need in order to ask the stupid questions and be willing to be proved wrong. I had a cautious faith in his idea—and absolute confidence that his mindset was a match for my own.

So began the second great bromance of my life. Don't tell Ben Affleck.

5

WATER.ORG
BEGINS

POV: Gary White

Matt Damon is great at telling stories. I know I'm probably the millionth person on the planet to have that thought, but it really was the first thing that struck me about him.

Not long before we met in the hotel ballroom at CGI, I'd sat in the audience as Matt took part in a panel discussion about the water crisis. For the most part, it was your average conversation about international development—which is to say it managed to be incredibly dry even when it touched on issues of literally life and death. Except when Matt was speaking. Whenever he had the mic, I could feel the energy in the room increase, feel the people around me sit up and pay attention. And yes, that might be because Matt is famous. But it might also be true that Matt is famous precisely *because* he has that effect on people. In any event, it was clear to me, clear to everyone in the room, that Matt brought a passion to these issues that was very deeply felt.

As the panel was wrapping up, the moderator asked Matt how it felt to do work that saves lives. I think we were all expecting him to give the typical celebrity do-gooder response about the importance of giving back, and to close the conversation by giving us all a nice pat on the back for our good work.

Matt had a different idea. He launched into a story about— and this is true—a cannibal living in Germany in 2003. Matt described the cannibal as a classic Hannibal Lecter type, with one key exception: *this* cannibal was looking for a willing victim. So he went online, wherever cannibals go on the internet to chat, and he asked if anybody out there would agree to be eaten. There was a shocking number of volunteers. So he sifted through their applications, found one he liked, and invited the guy to his house. To get to know each other, they had dinner and went out to a movie: *Ocean's Eleven*. Starring—you saw this coming—Matt Damon.

So the two guys saw the movie, and on their way out, the would-be victim turned to the cannibal and said, "I've changed my mind. I don't want you to eat me." They shook hands and parted ways.

"So," Matt said, "at least I know I've helped save *one* life."

As I got to know Matt over the coming months, I saw this happen again and again. Not his telling cannibalism stories (I think he has only one), but what he had done before that: get everyone's attention with a perfectly delivered story or statistic or insight, helping them find their passion for the issue by giving them access to his own. The guy is simply one of the best communicators I've ever seen.

And at that moment, an exceptional communicator was just what WaterPartners needed most. For all the progress we'd made, it had been a continual challenge to persuade people to care about the water crisis when, as Matt wrote earlier, they'd never been forced to imagine what it would be like to go without water. And as our approach evolved, telling our story became more and more complicated. Early on, we'd been able to tell potential donors that their contributions would help pay for a water system. That was pretty straightforward—easy to express, easy to understand. But now, our most powerful solution was harder to explain than the problem itself. Instead of "Help us pay for a water system," we were saying "Help us help microfinance institutions manage the risk of building water and sanitation lending portfolios." Not in so many words—but I'll tell you from experience, it was hard to do it in fewer or clearer words.

So I saw from the start how valuable a partner Matt would be in this work. And as we intensified our conversations over the next few months, I saw that he didn't just have an incredible knack for storytelling—he had a sharp mind for policy and strategy, a commitment to innovation, and a real seriousness of purpose about this work. If *People* magazine had a "Most Substantive Celebrity Alive" issue, he'd win the title hands down. Given the values we shared, and the different strengths we each brought to the table, I thought that if we joined up, we could do something really special.

But neither of us had been in this alone: we each led, and were accountable to, our own organizations. And before Matt and I could create a true partnership, we would have to make sure our colleagues saw our vision, too. Depending on your perspective and your degree of confidence in the other party, a merger can look like a sharing of strengths, or it can look like a sacrifice of identity and autonomy. Raising the idea with our respective organizations was like introducing two families before a marriage takes place, and both are a little skeptical about the union that's being proposed.

Frankly, our board at WaterPartners was nervous about Matt. How seriously, they wondered, was a celebrity going to take this unsexy work? Was he going to get bored by it and move on? I assured them that Matt was as serious about the work as I was and that he could (and did) spend hours talking about WaterCredit; but this didn't settle the issue. The board was also worried that Matt could end up in some big scandal and drag WaterPartners down with him. Nothing about Matt himself made the board worry about this; he always projected as a stand-up guy. It was just seen as an occupational hazard of working with celebrities. And it could prove costly. After Lance Armstrong confessed to cheating in 2013, his charity Livestrong was mocked as "LiveWrong" and "LieStrong."[1] In the years after the scandal, annual donations to the foundation fell from $41 million to $2.5 million.[2]

For what it was worth, I told them that based on my own impressions, Matt really did seem to be—as he himself puts it—an "aging suburban dad." Not everyone bought this description of Jason Bourne.

At Matt's organization, H$_2$O Africa, people were skeptical of me for precisely the opposite reason: outside the insular world of water and sanitation development, I was what you might call an anti-celebrity. Meaning: nobody knew who I was. I'd met some of Matt's partners at H$_2$O Africa before—they were the people who'd put me in touch with Matt—but the others needed convincing that our organization was the real deal. Matt and his partners vouched for me, just as I vouched for him. Fortunately, as all this was going on, I was named a Skoll Foundation Social Entrepreneur—one of the greatest honors of my life. Every year, the foundation—started by Jeff Skoll, the former president of eBay—puts thousands of social entrepreneurs through a rigorous analysis and gives awards to a few who they think are most likely to create system-level change in the world. That award gave the people at H$_2$O Africa—and me, by the way—greater confidence that WaterCredit really did have as much potential as Matt and I had been saying.

In time our professional families, as families often do, came around and embraced our union. Not reluctantly, but enthusiastically. By mid-2009, we were drawing up documents for the merger. Our new organization needed a new name. As we brainstormed about it, we kept coming back to Water.org—that URL I'd claimed over a decade ago. It wasn't flashy, but it got right to the point. If you want to take action against the water crisis, you'll know just where to go: Water.org. (If this reads like a plug, it is.)

We launched Water.org with a press release that July. I won't say that we didn't want attention, but we didn't want hype; a big gala launch with Matt's name on the marquee would, we thought, send the wrong kind of message. Plus, CGI was coming up. We thought it'd be fitting to introduce people to Water.org at that event—which meant we needed a Commitment to Action. As excited as Matt and I both were about WaterCredit, we decided that Water.org's first big project would be providing large grants to our local partners in Haiti, so they could work with communities to build water systems and toilets. The country was still struggling after the previous hurricane season, which killed nearly eight hundred people and destroyed countless homes and buildings. When we attended CGI in 2009, just over half of the people in Haiti had access to safe water, and not even a third of the country's urban areas had safe sanitation systems.[3] (And this was *before* the tragic 2010 earthquake destroyed much of the water and sanitation infrastructure that did exist. As one reporter described the situation after the earthquake, "Life for most people is a constant struggle for water.")[4] We knew that WaterCredit could make a bigger impact in the long run, but Haiti had an urgent need for these community water and sanitation systems, and Water.org could help.

We got the chance to announce our commitment on the main stage at CGI. In 2008, it had been one of the coolest days of my life just to sit down with Matt Damon—and then President Clinton—and talk about the water crisis. Almost exactly a year later, I was standing on a stage with both of them to announce that Water.org would help bring safe water and sanitation to fifty thousand people in Haiti.

One interesting thing about that announcement: if you look up the photos online, Matt looks like he's learned a little *too* much from President Clinton. Matt's suit is that stereotypical politician blue; his tie has red and blue stripes; he has an American flag pin on his lapel. He looks like he's about to start addressing people as "folks." Well, that wasn't an accident. At the time, Matt was playing a politician in *The Adjustment Bureau*. The movie's producers wanted footage of him with famous real-world politicians—and, of course, there were few better places to find them than CGI. So the filmmakers tagged along. During Water.org's announcement, they recorded Matt and me onstage shaking hands with Clinton, giving me a one-second cameo in the movie.

Matt brought the film crew around with him through the rest of the event. Their cameras were a little bigger than the ones the news crews carried, but they blended in pretty well. Whenever he ran into political icons, he'd ask if they were open to appearing in his upcoming film. Thus the days of intense meetings about combating the water crisis were punctuated by spur-of-the-moment movie scenes, with leaders like Jesse Jackson and John Podesta stopping by to talk political strategy. Former secretary of state Madeleine Albright used her on-camera moment with Matt to explain why everyone should pay attention to the countries that are typically ignored in discussions of geopolitical strategy.

People ask me all the time what it's like to work with a movie star. I don't have a great answer to that, because I've worked with only one, and in most respects this movie star is as normal as anyone you'll ever meet. But as that CGI trip goes to show, it's sometimes a little surreal.

After we launched Water.org, WaterCredit started growing fast. As I said, people just want to listen to Matt, and now, listening to Matt meant hearing our story. Once they were paying attention, we could share our proof, which was growing, that WaterCredit worked. In all my years at WaterPartners, we'd reached 335,000 people with safe water and/or sanitation. In 2012, just a few years after we created Water.org, we reached our first million.

With evidence mounting every day that these loan programs were successful, and with the Skoll Foundation's endorsement, it got easier to persuade major foundations to give us grants that allowed us to reach more people, more quickly, than ever before. The Michael & Susan Dell Foundation and Reckitt, one of the world's largest consumer health companies, each provided the funding to reach about 50,000 people with water and sanitation; the PepsiCo Foundation provided the funding to reach nearly 3 million; the Caterpillar and Ikea foundations each provided the funding to reach over 6 million.

In international development, ideas that work well in pilot programs often perform worse as they're implemented more widely. Not every success is scalable. But in our case, the opposite happened: WaterCredit worked better as it got bigger. As MFIs got more effective at managing loan programs and sent out more and more microloans, the repayment rate actually *climbed*. Today, out of every hundred people who take out these loans, *ninety-nine* pay them back, in full and on time.

To me, this wasn't just a validation of WaterCredit. It refuted the idea of a charity-only approach—both for fighting the water crisis and more generally.

I know it probably feels strange to see charity talked about in a negative way, and I should be clear that I'm not trying to disparage this work. Charity almost always comes from a good place, and it really does make life better for people. Charity has to be part of solving challenges as vast as the water crisis.

The problem comes, to my mind, when we look at people in poverty *only* as subjects of charity. When all we hear about people in poverty is that they need our help—when all we hear about the problems in their lives is that we need to step in and solve them—we're conditioned to see them as this mass of people who are powerless in the face of daunting challenges. Looking at them that way obscures their diversity—and blinds us to their power.

For example, I'm sure you've gotten requests to donate to help people who have "nothing." And to be fair, if you're making tens or hundreds of thousands of dollars in income a year, then people who make one or two or four dollars a day *do* seem like they're living on next to nothing. Any small differences in income appear minuscule—irrelevant, even.

But over the years, my conversations with people in poor communities have shown me just how much those differences matter. Going from making one dollar a day to two dollars a day is a 100 percent increase. A jump from two dollars to four dollars a day is, again, doubling your income. Just imagine how much your life would change if your salary doubled! Well, that jump changes life drastically for people in poverty as well. I've met people without access to clean water who can't even afford a second plastic bucket to collect water. I've also, as I've described, met people who are forced to shell out substantial amounts of money each day to buy dirty water from tanker trucks. In both cases, these people are trapped in poverty—but at different *levels* of poverty. So they are living very different lives.

If I were in the business world, I'd say we need to *segment the market*. There are of course people whose incomes (if they have incomes) are so very low that they can be reached only through charity. But when we focus only on them, we lose sight of just how many people out there are ready to fuel their own rise—if we'd just help clear the barriers standing in their way.

And that's a big missed opportunity—because when people in poverty are able to invest even a little bit in their own futures, they are experts at getting the maximum possible value out of that investment.

I saw this on my visits to the communities where Water-Credit was working. On these trips, I met women like Janine. Matt and I spoke with her when we visited the Philippines in

2019. She's a young mother of three who, like all of us, wants the best for her family—which requires her to be extremely strategic about every single financial move her family makes. When Janine's children were young, she made an incredible sacrifice: she moved to Bahrain so she could take a higher-paying job and send the money she made back home. Janine showed us a photo on her wall—a family photo taken just before she had left for Bahrain. Her daughter was a toddler, her face still showing her baby fat. By the time Janine was able to move back to the Philippines, her toddler had become a gangly child. I couldn't imagine how hard it must have been to miss out on those years of her child's life.

But Janine's sacrifice gave her family the start they needed. Once she settled back home, she got a series of small loans and paid them all back: loans to build her business selling groceries and delivering fresh meat, and then, when she'd paid back those loans, loans to build her family some decent living quarters, and then—at long last—a loan for a water connection. With each improvement, the family climbed further out of the depths of poverty. They had more money coming in, less money going out, and more time and energy to build the future they wanted.

I saw this same determination in every community I visited. I remember another woman I met in Ghana, Mama Florence Waswa, a mother and grandmother. She used to live on less than three dollars a day. She didn't have an opportunity to earn more, because she had to spend much of her time riding around on a bike to collect water for her family.

But then she got a $275 loan. With that money, she said, she was able to install a water pump and storage tank in her home. She's using the water to grow vegetables, and feeding some of the vegetables to pigs she's started to raise. She's also using the water to make bricks out of clay—and she's selling those, too. With her bricks, Mama Florence has also been able to add a few rooms onto her house, rooms that she rents out—another source of income. And with all that, she has enough water to spare that she can sell the surplus to her neighbors, earning money to send her grandchildren to school. Once she was freed of the burden of constantly searching for water, all that human potential came rushing out.

As I heard more and more stories like this, I saw that no matter where you are in the world, people have a fundamental drive to improve their lives. To build something better. I kept hearing people describe the plans they had for their families, all the sacrifices and investments they were making to improve their futures. They were just facing far greater barriers than most of us do in countries like the United States.

But in the Philippines and Ghana and around the world, so many people were surmounting these barriers. In these conversations, I'd hear about exciting business ideas, big plans for their kids' education, savings goals that were finally within reach. I'd see families wiring their houses for electricity, buying gas stoves so they didn't have to cook over open fires, building roofs that actually kept out the rain. I was seeing families lift themselves out of poverty.

This was part of a larger global shift. So many families had been lifting themselves out of poverty since I started this work in the 1980s that they were changing the world around them. I could see the change clearly because I'd spent decades visiting low-income countries. Often, I'd travel somewhere that I hadn't visited for five or ten years, and I'd find it almost unrecognizable: where there once had been slums or barren fields, there were now bustling streets, vibrant markets, apartment buildings. The world was transforming itself, right before my eyes. It was one of the most hopeful things I'd ever seen.

I think it can be hard to see or believe in this change because extreme poverty remains persistent, and it's wrenching to see it up close. It can sound naïve to talk about how much better things are getting when so many people are still suffering. But we can—and we need to—focus on both realities at the same time. Because the fact is, if we ignore the positive changes happening around us, then we're blinding ourselves to one of the most important stories of progress of our time.

The person who opened my eyes to this way of thinking was a Swedish physician and professor of global health named Hans Rosling, who passed away a few years ago. He spoke more clearly about poverty than anyone I've encountered and spent his life traveling the world to fight, as he put it, "devastating global ignorance."[5] Almost everywhere he went, he asked people a question: *In the last twenty years, would you say the proportion of the world population living in poverty has (a) almost doubled, (b) remained more or less the same, or (c) almost halved?*[6]

Worldwide, 93 percent of the twelve thousand people that

Rosling quizzed—in the United States it was 95 percent of those polled—answered a or b. Which means that nearly everybody everywhere was wrong. The correct answer is c: in the last twenty years, the percentage of people living in poverty has been cut in half. The communities where I was seeing such incredible growth weren't special cases; they were representative of change happening across the world. But almost no one was talking about this. As Rosling pointed out, a monkey—which would, of course, choose randomly—would do better at answering this question correctly than a human.[7]

Rosling said that the decline in extreme poverty is the most important change that has happened in the world during his lifetime. There is likely no single change that can reduce more suffering in a person's life than rising from extreme poverty. An end to extreme poverty means no more living through "hunger seasons" between harvests. It means no more dying of easily preventable diseases because you can't afford the most basic medicines. It means no more spending your life hauling buckets of dirty water from a faraway well.

And these transformations are happening at a staggering rate. As Oxford University researcher Max Roser put it a few years ago, "Newspapers could have had the headline 'Number of people in extreme poverty fell by 137,000 since yesterday' every day in the last 25 years."[8]

This means that in the coming decades, hundreds of millions of people will rise out of extreme poverty—and become a source of enormous economic growth. If we invest in them, they will continue to break the cycle of poverty and better their lives. And with every extra dollar they make, they have more power to fuel their rise.

When you start to see people in poverty in this way, it no longer makes sense to talk about them the way people in the rich world so often do—as a *problem to be solved*.

They start looking, instead, like a *market to be served*.

And that, we at Water.org realized, was the change in mindset we needed to help bring about. We want people in wealthy nations to stop talking about struggling communities as if they are helpless—as if their only chance at a better future is through our sympathy and charity. We want everyone to see their potential; respect their strength, ambition, and initiative; and help them harness their power.

President Clinton, who'd known Water.org from the beginning, was always excited to hear our updates and see our latest results. He completely understood the idea and its potential, and a few years after we launched our organization, he gave us a piece of advice that is still a mantra for us: "Keep running those numbers up," he said. "Just keep running those numbers up."

And that's what we did. We were beginning to prove that we were not just another water NGO seeking incremental change. We were in the business of innovation, the business of pioneering better solutions, scalable solutions. And we knew that in order to do that successfully, we had to get these solutions working so well and in so many places that no one could ignore them. So we made the painful decision to end our work on subsidized community water projects. By then, that model was being pursued by countless other water NGOs—and we knew that we could reach vastly more people by focusing our energies on WaterCredit.

Making breakthroughs and running up our numbers required a great deal of hard work from our whole team. In the early days, everyone was a volunteer—starting with me—who at one point or another did every job. But real innovation requires hiring top talent. Hiring that talent can be financially challenging for an NGO, but as our impact grew, more donors were coming on board, and our revenue was growing. We were also gaining a reputation as a team of innovators that was disrupting the water charity paradigm. This helped us in recruiting people with passion, commitment, and skill. I created the position of president and hired Jennifer Schorsch, a supersmart and committed Harvard MBA, to fill it. We started building a team—which now has more than 130 people—with diverse skills, including deep expertise in finance and microfinance.

With such a strong team helping us grow, we found new partners in new places. As we expanded across the globe, we learned from MFI and banking leaders like Kamrul Tarafder in the Philippines, Ana Maria Zegarra Leyva in Peru, and James Mwangi in Kenya. Incredible experts all, and they helped us adapt the model to different contexts.

We started to move really, really fast. I began feeling a lot like I had in the eighties when I started this work—feeling as if we really could, someday soon, end the water crisis for good. But this time it wasn't the naïveté of youth. This time, my biggest, boldest ambitions were grounded in actual evidence. Publicly, though, I knew we needed to be a little more restrained than that, more buttoned-up and responsible, if we wanted to stay credible. So anytime Matt or I got a little too excited in an interview or on a panel about the progress we thought we could make, we'd give each other a kind of . . . *warning* look.

After seeing how quickly these communities were transforming themselves, though, I found it harder and harder to contain my own enthusiasm. I remember holding a strategy meeting around this time—board members, consultants, the whole complement. There were about twenty people in the room. At some point, someone asked what we would identify as Water.org's most important goal. Without thinking, I blurted out the goal that Matt and I had been talking about in private. "We want to solve the water crisis—*in our lifetimes*," I said.

Total silence.

Lynn Taliento, our brilliant board chair at the time, shot Matt a look that said: *This guy is insane.* And as I looked at him, I saw him give me *that look.* There was some awkward laughter. No one's was more awkward than mine. Then someone asked: "Well, whose lifetime are we talking about? Who's the youngest, healthiest person here?" Suddenly we were having a serious conversation about actuarial tables and whether we could actually map this out on a timeline. Which hadn't really been my aim. What I was trying to say was that, yes, solving the world's water crisis was an audacious goal, but it wasn't a distant, fantastical goal. It wasn't going to require some big technological leap—like finding a cure for cancer or for AIDS. Nor was it going to take a major diplomatic push, negotiations, painful concessions—like those needed to solve the Israeli-Palestinian conflict. What it was going to take was, first, a recognition that it was possible, and, second, the resources to make it possible.

No small thing, in either case. But when you start to look at things this way, it no longer seems irresponsible to suggest we can get this done in our lifetime. It starts to seem irresponsible to suggest otherwise. It starts to look like a lack of imagination—or a failure of will—to say that we can't do it.

Eventually, my off-the-cuff comment became the title of the white paper that resulted from these strategy sessions. We called the paper "In Our Lifetime." And from that point forward, it has defined Water.org's main goal. Our mission is not just to address the global water crisis. Our mission—in our lifetime—is to help solve it for good.

6

THE BIG IDEA, TAKE TWO

POV: Matt Damon

It was August 2013, and Gary and I were several hours into a long drive across southeastern India, feeling frustrated. And not just because of the traffic.

Usually, our trips to the communities where WaterCredit was working were full of joy. We'd talk to women who'd taken out water and sanitation loans and learn what they were doing with the extra hours in their days. We'd visit schools and sing along with the kids: *"This is the way we brush our teeth, brush our teeth, brush our teeth. This is the way we brush our teeth, so early in the morning."* We'd meet with the microfinance institutions and hear them report the same good news, every time: the loans were being repaid at a rate of about 99 percent.

But on this trip, the atmosphere at some of the MFIs was different. Which was not a total surprise. For months now, we'd been hearing that the loan programs weren't reaching as many people as we thought they could. Repayment rates weren't the problem. So what was it? We needed to figure it out.

Every time we met with an MFI on that trip, we asked the same question: "What's the biggest obstacle in your way right now?" Almost word for word, they all gave the same answer: "Consistent access to affordable capital."

One of the biggest challenges MFIs face is keeping their loans affordable for people. Vetting and administering a $200 loan doesn't take any less effort than doing the same for a $20,000 loan, and inflation is high in most of the countries where we work. So for MFIs to recoup their costs and make a reasonable profit, they often have to charge higher interest than they'd like.

For the most part, MFIs had figured out how to navigate these challenges. The problem arose when the MFIs tried to meaningfully expand the number of water and sanitation loans they gave out—which was of course the point. To do that, the MFIs needed more money, and not the kind of money they might have stashed away in a safe somewhere in the back. Like, a lot more money. The kind of money you can get only from a big commercial bank. But the big banks just didn't understand how people in poverty were going to pay back loans that failed to generate income. They were new to this whole idea. So they put a high price on their risk, and insisted on charging the MFIs really high interest—around 15 percent.

So now, if the MFIs were going to pay the costs of administering the loans, pay back the big banks, and make a small profit, they were going to have to charge their customers—some of the poorest people on the planet—an interest rate of about 25 percent. At that point, many borrowers start to be priced out of the market. I'm sure you've heard people say not to take on credit card debt unless you have no other choice, because the interest rates are so high. Well, on average, credit card companies in the United States charge *16 percent* interest.[1]

The MFIs were trying to lift people up, not bury them in debt. So if they couldn't get their interest rates lower soon, most of them would stop making new loans.

"Consistent access to affordable capital." That's what they kept telling us. That's what they needed. Until the MFIs could find an ample source of money they could afford to borrow, there was going to be a serious limit on how many loans they could offer.

The whole reason Gary and I had been so excited about WaterCredit—and the whole reason we'd felt bold enough to talk about ending the crisis for good—was that we thought we could get to a point where these loans would be available to everyone who needed one. But here, already, we seemed to be hitting a ceiling. We knew we'd never break through it unless we could find some way to get these MFIs a steady stream of affordable capital.

When Gary and I started working together, we adopted a rule that Ben Affleck once established for our screenwriting sessions: "Judge me on how good my good ideas are, not how bad my bad ideas are." So as Gary and I were sitting in the back of a jeep in India, I felt free to suggest what I thought might be a very bad idea: "If these MFIs can't get affordable capital," I said, "why can't we just raise it for them?"

When I was growing up, my dad, Kent Damon, was a stockbroker—so when it came to finance, I knew, as they say, just enough to be dangerous. It seemed to me that there was an enormous pool of money out there that we ought to be able to tap into. The amount of money that institutions across the world donate to development assistance each year is about $161 billion.[2] Which is a lot. Except that the amount of capital sitting in global markets is about $250 *trillion*.[3] That's a lot more. It is, in fact, over 1,500 times more. Nonprofits aren't in the habit of thinking about that kind of money, because it's investment capital—money that is supposed to generate a financial return. The money that people (as well as corporate philanthropies) donated to Water.org had no such expectation attached. The whole idea of philanthropic giving is that it's, well, *giving*. You give it away to help improve people's lives and never expect to get it back. But why couldn't we ask people and organizations to contribute differently to our work? What about asking some of them not to give the money away, but to invest it, and to get a modest return on that investment?

Gary was aware that some other organizations had started doing the same thing—funding their work with investment capital. He didn't know if we'd be able to pull that off, but he didn't see any reason why we *couldn't*. Neither did I. As I told Gary, I was confident there were investors who'd accept some risk and lower returns for the guarantee of improving people's lives. I mean, I'd do it. Which, I realized, might actually be a start. So I said: "If we can make this work, I'll be the first to invest."

On one of the last nights of the trip, we hosted a dinner in Bangalore with some leaders of Indian MFIs. Gary asked them: "If we could get you capital at half the price you're paying for it now, how many people could you reach?"

One of the officials said, "Twice as many."

Gary asked, "How soon could you start?"

This answer came quickly, too. "Tomorrow."

◊

If you're lucky enough to have money in the bank that you don't need to spend anytime soon, and you're looking to do something with it, many people see two choices: either give some of it away to a nonprofit, using it to do good in the world; or invest it in the market and do some good, hopefully, for your own finances. In the first case, you're accepting zero returns. In the second, you're looking for maximum returns.

What Gary and I were proposing didn't really fit into either of those categories. On the one hand, it wasn't charitable or philanthropic giving; on the other, it wasn't the kind of investment that aims to make the greatest returns possible. What we were describing was something in-between. Which didn't strike us as a radical idea. There ought to be a wide middle ground between those two approaches—shouldn't there? But as we began to road test the idea—sounding it out with smart people in the worlds of philanthropy and finance—we got the sense that it wasn't an easy sell. The divide between *giving* and *investing* seemed to many like an apples and oranges thing, and in our naïveté, we were trying to pitch people on, I don't know, an apple-orange.

I probably would have expected this response if I'd been familiar at the time with a best-selling book called *Predictably Irrational*. Its author, a behavioral economist named Dan Ariely, argues that each of us lives by two sets of very different norms—and we switch sets of norms depending on the situation. There are *social norms*, where our instinct is to be giving, to be selfless, to make sure people get what they need.[4] And then there are *market norms*, where our instinct is to be efficient, to be self-reliant, to get the maximum personal benefit for the minimum personal sacrifice.[5] Because market norms and social norms have competing priorities, it's difficult to live by both of these norms at the same time. So, instead, we sort of toggle between them. And as Ariely puts it: "Once the market norms enter our considerations, the social norms depart."[6]

There are plenty of examples of this. One that Ariely describes is how AARP, which wanted to provide affordable legal services to retirees, asked lawyers to help by reducing their rate to thirty dollars per hour. There were no takers. But then AARP changed tactics: it asked the lawyers to offer their services pro bono. Suddenly lots of lawyers offered their services for free. If they didn't want to do the work for thirty dollars an hour, why would they do it for nothing? Because AARP—without knowing it—had taken its request out of the realm of market norms (where it sounded to the lawyers like a terrible deal) and put it in the realm of social norms (where it sounded like a noble use of their time).[7]

Since we're not very good at living by both sets of norms at once, they occupy entirely different spheres. Businesses, of course, celebrate the profit motive while nonprofits celebrate, well, the nonprofit motive. Sometimes you see the same divide *within* a foundation: you've got one group of people, one subculture, responsible for managing the foundation's investments and expanding its endowment, and a separate group in charge of giving the money away. This can lead to some really strange scenarios, like foundations that invest their money in fossil fuel companies that pollute the environment, then give the profits to organizations that fight climate change.

Examples like that one aside, this all seems fine on its face. Businesses (and investments in businesses) make money, philanthropies give it away. But it's not fine. The result is a massive misallocation of resources. If that $250 trillion of investment capital is basically off-limits to the organizations working to do good in the world—if all we're working with is the $195 billion spent every year on development assistance—then we're trying to solve the world's most difficult problems with just 0.08 percent of its resources.[8] Not a formula for success.

But it ought to be possible to care about your own well-being and the world's future at the same time. On this point, let me reintroduce you to an authority I cited earlier: my mom, Nancy Carlsson-Paige.

When I was in college, she had a list of areas that she wouldn't invest in because they were harmful—businesses that polluted the environment were obvious ones, or companies that had committed human rights violations. I remember thinking that it was a great idea, but—as is often the case with kids and their parents—years went by before I realized how ahead of her time she was. (I've stressed this point to my own kids, so far with limited success.) Not until Gary and I started looking into finance did I realize that my mom was part of an early wave of what would later be known as "impact investing."

Impact investing started with something called divestment, which is what my mom was doing in her own portfolio: screening investments to get the unethical stuff out. Some religious denominations, like Quakers and Methodists, had in effect been doing this since the 1700s, when they urged against profiting from slavery and war.[9] But the idea didn't go mainstream until the late 1960s, when universities, unions, and nonprofits started looking at their investments through a more critical lens,[10] withdrawing investments from companies that sold things like tobacco and firearms.[11] The movement kind of flew under the radar until the mid-1980s, when activists started pressuring investors to take their money out of South African businesses during the time of apartheid. By the time I was in college, students had made headlines for staging protests and getting arrested—with the goal of getting their universities to divest.[12] Faith communities, state and city governments, and labor unions pulled their money out of South Africa and called on big companies, banks, and the US government to do the same.[13] By the early nineties, over $20 billion had been divested from corporations that did business in South Africa—and the economic impact was so profound that some think it pressured the South African government to participate in negotiations that, over time, ended apartheid.[14]

That emboldened the movement to think even bigger. It was one thing (and an important thing) to stop investing in repressive regimes, unethical companies, and dangerous products. But what about the flip side of that coin—what about promoting investments in good things? I don't mean good products—there's never been a shortage of investment in companies that build a better whatever. I mean investing in solutions to the world's biggest challenges. Maybe that was never going to generate the kind of returns you'd see from buying stock in, say, Apple ahead of the launch of the iPhone. But what if you could get a decent return while putting your money to work toward creating a better, fairer, safer world?

This is where a woman named Judith Rodin comes in. In 2005, Rodin—the former president of the University of Pennsylvania—was appointed to run the Rockefeller Foundation. Going all the way back to the original Rockefeller, John D., the family name has been shorthand for having tons of money. But when Rodin took the helm, she couldn't help but notice the *lack* of money. Don't get me wrong: the foundation's assets would be a dream come true for an organization like Water.org—or really almost any nonprofit. But when Rodin compared them with the scale of the problems her foundation was trying to solve, they suddenly looked pretty paltry.

Five years earlier, nearly every nation in the world signed on to the UN Millennium Development Goals. The goals were ambitious—among them, countries pledged to end hunger and make sure that every child in the world received a primary education—so the goals had a big price tag. By some estimates it would take between $82 billion and $152 billion in additional development financing each year to reach the goals by 2015.[15] Numbers like these revealed a huge and urgent funding gap: to meet the goals, nations would need to essentially double their foreign aid budgets. You didn't have to be a finance minister to know this wasn't in the cards.

And foundations like the Rockefeller Foundation, no matter how big their endowments were, couldn't come close to filling the gap. The Rockefeller Foundation awarded about $100 million in grants every year.[16] The Gates Foundation, biggest of them all, was giving about $1.35 billion in annual grants at the time.[17] Even if it had all been directed at the Millennium Development Goals (MDGs)—and it wasn't—it wouldn't have qualified as a down payment. The world needed another solution.

So Judith Rodin went to work on finding one. In the summer of 2007, she and her team gathered a group of investors, philanthropists, and entrepreneurs in a beautiful villa overlooking Lake Como in northern Italy.[18] The villa had been donated to the foundation a long time ago by an Italian princess—because that's the kind of thing that happens when your name is Rockefeller.[19] The foundation has used it for decades to bring creative thinkers together and help them advance their work. Rodin gave her summer gathering a clear mission: figure out how to mobilize more capital for social and environmental good.

The group believed that at least some of the people who controlled the world's capital could be persuaded to prioritize these kinds of investments. But they figured that if this practice was really going to take off, it needed a name. They coined the term *impact investing*. They also saw that for this movement to grow, it needed some degree of organization, so the Rockefeller Foundation set up a network where impact investors could get together, work together, and trade ideas. And the group realized that if they were going to convince more financiers to invest for impact as well as profit, they'd need a way of measuring impact just as rigorously as investors measure returns. So the foundation helped establish a Global Impact Investing Rating System. GIIRS grades each fund's overall performance, like any other rating system, but this one also rates funds on how their investments impact, say, the environment, or the lives of the people in a community.[20]

That meeting set some powerful forces in motion. As the decade progressed, more and more impact-oriented funds sprang up, and more and more investors began to cite this as a priority. Eleven years after the meeting at the lake, a report described the shift: what had once been a small, disruptive movement was now "a complex and rich investment ecosystem."[21]

Of course, Gary and I were not only new to the world of impact investing—we were new to the world of investing, period. We talked to pretty much everyone we knew in the financial sector, and a bunch of people we hadn't known. We asked them the same naïve question Gary had asked in the early days of WaterCredit: Why wouldn't this work?

The first person I talked to was my dad. I think a lot of fathers dream of the moment when their kid comes home and says: "Dad, tell me about your work." I'm sure my dad and I had had those conversations when I was growing up, but to be honest, I can't say I grasped the concepts. So when I started again, in my forties, to ask my dad about his work, it felt like new territory. When I explained Gary's and my idea to him, I expected him to shoot it down, to tell me (gently) why it couldn't possibly work. But he didn't. He thought about it awhile. Then he told me he believed it *could* work. In order for an impact investment to be successful, you need both solid returns and reliable, impressive numbers validating that the investment can change lives. The investment we were proposing would meet both of those tests.

Hearing my dad get excited about our idea was incredibly encouraging—but as he cautioned, we had a lot of issues to address. Gary and I were still learning the basic vocabulary of finance—back then, if you'd asked me what a capital stack was, I'd have pictured a pile of dollar bills. We also had to struggle our way through complexities like currency manipulation, tax laws for nonprofits (laws that, in a lot of cases, varied by country), and the difficulty of getting capital in and out of places like India. Gary and I gave serious thought to urging actual experts to run with the idea while we cheered from the sidelines.

But our experience with WaterCredit encouraged us to try to prove our own case—to get things going in a modest way, build from there, and, as Bill Clinton had advised us, keep "running those numbers up" until no one could ignore them.

Luckily, we had built a highly skilled team at Water.org that understood water and sanitation markets and microfinance. Our former chief operating officer, Keith Stamm, who had worked with private equity investors, came back to help us put together a plan—to help us figure out what that mutant apple-orange would actually look like. We decided to start with a $10 million fund and to set a target of a 2 percent return. A fund of that scale could bring clean water or sanitation to over 730,000 people.

Our board was nervous about it, for good reason. This was a radical departure for us. As I mentioned earlier, the world had just been burned by bad actors in the financial crisis. We knew that even if we had the most noble intentions, we could be in big trouble if we messed up. If the fund failed, it could drag Water.org's credibility down with it—and put us at the mercy of government regulators and the Securities and Exchange Commission. So here was a test—a high-stakes test—of our commitment to the bold vision (or big talk) of just a few years earlier, when Gary and I had convinced our board that the goal of ending the water crisis in our lifetimes was actually within reach. Now Gary and I had convinced each other, at least, that having made this bold claim, we couldn't shrink from taking the risks that could make it a reality.

Our board, in the end, agreed. Emphatically. When the moment came to make a decision, someone turned to our board chair, Lynn Taliento, and said, "Are we going to do this?"

And Lynn replied: "Fuck, yeah."

But market forces weren't the only reason that MFIs found it so hard to get affordable capital. Governments had some responsibility here, too. In India, the central bank—India's equivalent of the Federal Reserve—has a policy called Priority Sector Lending, which, done right, is smart policy. It requires banks to allocate a certain percentage of their loans to key sectors—priority areas like education, agriculture, and small business. All of which is fine, except that water and sanitation weren't considered a priority sector. And that, for the MFIs, was a big problem. The banks lending to the MFIs would have to charge higher rates for any nonpriority loans. Even for water and sanitation loans to people in poverty.

Now, I know that a lot of people think celebrities should keep out of politics, and stay even further away from policymaking, but I will say that I don't make it a habit to try to change the policies of countries on the other side of the world. (It's not as if my track record in changing policies in the United

States is so great.) But Gary and I believed we had to find a way to change that priority lending policy. It wasn't just failing to prioritize water and sanitation loans—it was penalizing them. Ironically, India was undercutting one of its biggest goals before it even got launched: the Indian government was about to announce a five-year, $20 billion campaign to end open defecation. Not reduce it, but end it. Water.org's India team, led by our incredible colleagues P. Uday Shankar and Pon Aananth, spearheaded an effort to persuade the central bank to put water and sanitation on the priority list. Which is how I ended up in a conference room at the Reserve Bank of India, lobbying the bank to change its lending policy. If I was wondering what I was doing there, I'm sure I wasn't alone.

I don't know how much I contributed that day, especially compared with our India team and others in India championing water and sanitation. But all that mattered was that the effort succeeded. It didn't happen overnight, but eventually the Reserve Bank of India put water and sanitation on its list of priority sectors. India had become a proving ground for us in many ways, allowing us to test new ideas that, if they succeeded, could expand to other countries around the world. We could feel the momentum building—and we knew the time was right to start pitching our fund.

◊

Gary and I began turning up at conferences and in offices where you were pretty unlikely to find an actor or a water and sanitation engineer: international finance meetings, investment banks. We also showed up in Davos, Switzerland, at the World Economic Forum, where global elites pay shocking sums of money to visit a ritzy ski village and talk about the scourge of income inequality. Earlier I wrote about the Clinton Global Initiative meeting in New York. This is like that, but in $2,000 fur-trimmed ski jackets. As you might expect, people tend to kick the event around a lot. One of the best descriptions of Davos I've heard is that it's "where billionaires tell millionaires what the middle class feels."[22] You can be confident this is accurate, because the person who shared that insight is billionaire Jamie Dimon.

Davos is a tempting target. Self-awareness, in the thin mountain air, is in short supply. But there is something to be said—and I'll go ahead and say it—for gathering some of the most powerful people in the world to talk about the most pressing issues in the world and to see how, together, they might use their power to improve things. So Gary and I practiced our pitch and went to the Alps. We made the rounds—which, at Davos, involves a lot of short, down-to-business meetings in hotel lobbies and in storefronts converted into corporate hospitality suites (come for the hot chocolate, stay for the talk about strategies to meet our 2030 sustainability targets). We talked to anyone who would listen about the water crisis, about a solution that was working, and about tapping new sources of capital to really bring it to scale. The world's poor, we said, are willing to buy in with what little resources they have. With all the wealth we have, are we?

The answer, judging by the blank looks we got, was no. We're not. People were very nice to Gary and me: they put us on panels; gave us an award; listened when we gave speeches and applauded when we were done. But we did not seem to be winning converts. We got a lot of nodding and smiling and "keep us posted," but no commitments. Which mystified me. Many of these leaders and the organizations they ran were happy to donate millions to worthy causes (including ours). And here we were, offering them a chance for their money to have an even greater impact and, at the same time, to earn a return on investment, and they just weren't interested. I can see now that we were tripping over that divide between social norms and market norms. People saw Water.org, rightly enough, as an NGO, and no one *invests* in NGOs; they *give* to NGOs. Some people said outright: "I do philanthropy with my philanthropy, and I make money with my money." Others represented institutions that were geared (even required) to minimize financial risk and maximize financial return. Either way, we were coming up empty.

On the last night of the conference, Gary and I were sitting around the chalet where we were staying, feeling let down. I kept replaying in my head all the words I'd heard about reducing inequality and being good global citizens. Was it all just talk—the critics' knock on Davos?

The person who showed up to comfort us was Bono. Well, *comfort* is not quite the right word. Because he took one look at me and started laughing. Davos was not my usual scene, so I'd tried to dress the part. I'm embarrassed to admit this, but I was wearing a sweater vest with a tie. Bono thought this was so funny that he took a picture of my neckline.

So we laughed at me for a while. But the truth was that I did feel kind of dejected. Like Gary, I was so excited by the idea of our fund that I guess I expected everyone to embrace it. I thought the impact investment movement had enough of a head of steam that our timing was perfect. But now it was clear that if our plan was going to work at all, it was going to be a tougher sell—a harder slog—than I'd anticipated. "How do you keep doing this?" I asked Bono. For two decades now, he'd been pushing governments, foundations, and companies to join the fight against poverty and disease, and while he and his allies had achieved some big successes, it was still an uphill battle. How did he keep his energy from flagging? He indulged me for a minute, agreeing that the work was hard. But then he gave me some tough love. You've got to be tenacious, he said. You've got to be relentless. I had the feeling he'd given himself this pep talk before.

Bono knows when to be a pest, but he also knows when to be a friend. A week later, he sent me an email. And there, as I opened it, was that photo of my sweater vest. The email also included a poem he'd written about our conversation. I lost the email years ago, which is really too bad—a Bono original, gone forever. I'm not an Irish poet, so I won't try to re-create it for you. But as someone with almost an English degree—honest, I've got most of the credits toward one—I'm nearly qualified to tell you what it was about. Its message was that you can't let yourself feel so burdened by the way the world is right now that you don't push it to become something different. And that if you did keep pushing—if we all kept pushing—then eventually the world would move.

7

THE WORLD MOVES

POV: Gary White

Bono, it turns out, was right: the world *did* move, and more quickly than we expected. Matt and I kept showing up at Davos every couple of years—and every time we went, people seemed more open to what we had to say. A pitch that had gotten polite nods at our first Davos trip was generating enthusiastic interest and follow-up questions by our second. By our third, it was generating follow-you-down-the-hall-and-ask-you-more-questions questions.

Either Matt and I were getting better at this, or the business world, for reasons having nothing to do with us, got more willing to listen. Actually, both things were probably true. We also had plenty of evidence that our model worked, and now we had the teams in place to keep scaling it up. And like non-native speakers who immerse themselves in a culture, Matt and I were learning the language and starting to feel our fluency in talking about finance.

At the same time, we were also aware that the broader conversation about the role and responsibilities of the private sector was evolving. Some of the titans of global capitalism were still a little shaky after the financial collapse of 2008–2009 and were getting worried—for good reason—that there was more trouble ahead, not just economically but in terms of their societal standing, their "social license to operate," as CEOs put it.

By 2016, two formidable challenges were keeping the capitalists (and almost everybody else, for that matter) awake at night. The first was climate change: scientists' warnings were becoming more and more dire. And the second was inequality—the stark reality that the global economic system was working only for the lucky few, leaving people at the base of the pyramid struggling to meet their most basic needs. Of course, these were not new problems. But it's one thing to be aware of a problem, another to do something about it, and a whole other thing to transform the way you think and do business in order to do something about it. That takes time.

For a long time, inequality and climate change had been the two big elephants in every room. It took work to ignore them—and believe me, some businesses worked pretty hard. But by the mid-2010s, it was not only harder to do that, it had become more obviously self-defeating. Scientific models predicted massive environmental and economic destruction over the next half century if businesses didn't radically change their behavior. The societal disruption would be so profound that in many places, companies would no longer have stable markets for their products. (To be clear: I'm putting this in the past tense because I'm looking back, but scientists are still saying the same thing, with increasing intensity.) That disruption, in fact, had already begun: populist political movements, which questioned (and were prepared to shake) the foundations of global capitalism, were gaining power around the world.

So were young people—not political power, just yet, but economic power. In 2016, millennials became the largest generation in the American workforce.[1] Members of this younger generation are especially concerned about climate change, inequality, and a wide range of other issues, and their values have helped drive their decisions about where to work, what to buy, and what to invest in, once they've earned enough money to invest. They're drawn to companies that align with their values. And as millennials have moved into adulthood, they've given business leaders a greater incentive (or push) to take on major social and environmental issues.

So the divisions between those two separate worlds that Matt just described—the for-profit and the not-for-profit, the worlds of market norms and social norms—started to blur in some positive ways. Also good news: I was hearing a whole lot less about that theory of capitalism that emerged in the 1970s and became, over time, like holy writ—the idea that a company's sole responsibility is to create value for its shareholders. Not its *main* responsibility, its *sole* responsibility. Instead, more and more, I was hearing business leaders say things like this: "To prosper over time, every company must not only deliver financial performance, but also show how it makes a positive contribution to society." This wasn't coming from the fringes. The person who said it is Larry Fink, CEO of BlackRock, the world's largest asset manager; Fink is one of the most influential people in finance.

Now, let's not get crazy here. I'm not claiming that all the CEOs of multinational corporations had some great, collective awakening, and we all lived happily ever after under cleaner skies. I remain plenty skeptical every time I hear from a vitamin company or a sunglasses company or a shoe company how they are changing the world.

But here's what I do know. As the conversation in the business world changed, it no longer seemed so radical to consider the impact an investment was going to make on the world, not just on the investor's portfolio.

We saw this firsthand as we tried to raise money. Finding investors for that first $10 million fund was a slog. It took a couple of years, and in the end, most of our investments ended up coming from foundations like Skoll and Hilton, from our board members, and from other individuals, such as Michael and Xochi Birch. For organizations that already work toward a social mission in *spending* their money, it's not too big a leap to work toward that same mission while *investing* it.

But as we closed that first fund, we encountered more and more openness, in more and more places, to investing in ideas like ours. Looking at the data, that's no big surprise. In 2012, there was $25 billion committed to impact investments.[2] Over the six years that followed, that number ballooned to *$500 billion*.[3] The total assets invested around the world grew by 20 percent over that period—while assets invested in impact investing funds grew by *2,000 percent*.[4] That apple-orange hybrid was having its moment.

There was another consequence, too, of the focus on inequality and climate change: people got more interested in water. A lack of clean water is about as stark an example of inequality as you can find, and water issues are central to the climate crisis, too. Though when it comes to climate, things get complicated.

Headlines tell the story. Headlines like "A Quarter of Humanity Faces Looming Water Crises."[5] Or "Water Shortages to Be Key Environmental Challenge of the Century, NASA Warns."[6] The thing to note about these headlines is that they're about the future, not the present. And that's where the complication comes in. For years I'd been hoping that journalists and other powerful people would finally start talking about the water crisis. At long last, they were doing just that. But the water crisis they were talking about was a *different* one—a future crisis, when supplies run dry—not the present crisis that billions of people are facing today.

Of course, it's crucial that the world focus on this issue. As someone who has spent his entire life fighting to make sure everyone gets access to water, I'm terrified by the prospect of a future where billions of people across the world struggle with water scarcity. We have to start planning for it now.

But the more I've learned about potential water shortages, the more concerned I've become that people might think that increasing people's access to water will actually *worsen* the coming crisis by reducing supplies further. This makes sense on its face—but it isn't the case. The first thing to understand about water shortages is that they're local, not global. This is different than, say, oil shortages. There's a global oil market; there isn't a global water market (notwithstanding bottles of Fiji water). Nor will there ever be in any meaningful way. There are a lot of barrels of oil being shipped around the world, but you couldn't begin to build a fleet big enough to carry the volume of water that a country uses even in a single day. So water is, and will remain, a local commodity. In that sense, increasing people's access to water in Indonesia isn't going to affect the water supply in California.

In fact—and this is the second thing to know about water usage—household consumption of water has relatively little effect on overall supplies. The vast majority of water that humanity uses doesn't go to households. Globally, about 70 percent of the fresh water that humans use goes to agriculture; 19 percent goes to industry.[7] Only 11 percent is used by households.[8] And families in poverty use less water than richer households do; families in poverty aren't using their water to take care of sprawling suburban lawns.[9] Solving the current water crisis by connecting those living in poverty is not going to worsen the other water crisis we will face in the future.

It's actually the opposite: the steps we take to address today's crisis should help prepare us for tomorrow's. When a family gets a rainwater collection system, for example, they can store water for the times when rain doesn't fall, and, therefore, better cope with the unpredictability. When more people get connected to water utilities, they're tapped into the infrastructure that, even in the worst of times, is more reliable than going it alone will ever be. And when the utility invests in improvements, the whole community can benefit, including its poorest sections.

The poorest households are the ones that need these investments in resiliency the most—because when water shortages happen, as they inevitably will (and already are) in some regions, the poorest people are hit the hardest. Imagine if your only water source is hours away—and it goes dry. Or if you rely on rainfall to grow crops to feed your family, and the rains don't come. Today in sub-Saharan Africa, more than 90 percent of people in rural areas depend on agriculture for their income, and more than 95 percent of farming depends on rainfall instead of irrigation systems.[10]

A few of our team members once went to visit Tigray, a region in northern Ethiopia. The hillsides there are dotted with specks of yellow—the jerricans women carry as they search for water. Most make a two- to three-hour journey for water every single day. Some of the women told our colleagues that the landscape used to be a lot greener—before the trees were cut down to make room for crops, and before climate change made the rainfall less frequent.

Our team asked the women where their grandmothers and great-grandmothers used to walk to get water—the same spots? Actually, the women of Tigray replied, their ancestors didn't have to go anywhere—water sources used to be plentiful right there in the village. The holes are all dried up now, forcing the women to go far and wide to find alternatives—or causing them to search for water by digging beneath the parched surface where ponds once existed and rivers once flowed. This daunting situation has been worsened by the terrible conflict in Tigray today.

When future water shortages hit, they're going to affect places like Tigray the most. Of course, those of us in wealthy nations are hardly immune to climate change—nobody is—but we do have the resources to address supply problems. We can build desalinization plants, for example, turning salt water into potable water; we can build wastewater treatment facilities to recycle the water we use. But in less developed countries, the poorest people will have three basic choices when supplies dry up. They can try to function with less and less water—and pay a toll in sickness and maybe even mortality. Or they can fight their neighbors over dwindling water supplies. We've seen this happen already in places like Darfur. Or, most likely, they can flee, becoming water refugees, searching for a home or a haven that has enough water for their families.

These mass migrations are of course hugely destabilizing

A wonderful friendship.

Gary in the Philippines on one of the engineering
service trips he organized during college.

The fundraiser in Kansas City, Missouri, where it all began.

The first makeshift WaterPartners office. Note the toilet on the left. Whether that was Gary trying to reinvent the toilet or a renovation gone awry, we couldn't tell you.

One of the early WaterPartners projects in Guatemala—learning how to build projects not *for* a community but *with* a community.

Zambia, 2006—the trip arranged by Bono's organization. Here, Matt found his passion for taking on the water crisis.

A young woman carrying water in Ethiopia. Jerricans like these weigh nearly forty pounds when full.

In costume as a politician (note the rep tie) for *The Adjustment Bureau*, Matt gives a speech at the real-life CGI.

Celebrating the creation of Water.org with President Clinton at the 2009 Clinton Global Initiative (CGI) Annual Meeting.

CGI's goal is to turn "ideas into action." For us, it did exactly that. Returning five years after we first met there, we shared how Water.org had reached millions with water and/or sanitation.

Dancing with school kids in Puliyambakkam Village in India.

Talking with a WaterCredit borrower in India. In India alone, WaterCredit loans have reached more than 15 million people with water and/or sanitation.

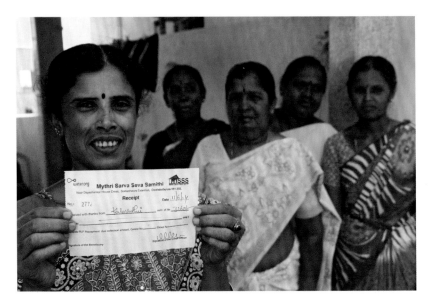

Kalavathi, a borrower from India, proudly displaying her loan card. This small loan will mean a big transformation for her family.

Messing around during the toilet strike shoot. Clearly, we'll do almost anything to get people to pay attention to this issue.

Breaking character during the toilet strike press conference.

Meeting with former World Bank president Jim Yong Kim in Washington, DC. Dr. Kim immediately saw how WaterCredit could help close the financing gap at the heart of the global water crisis.

Talking with Shereen Bhan of CNBC at the World Economic Forum in 2017. To raise the capital we need to take on the crisis, we go where the money is— and that's Davos.

Visiting the Philippines just before Christmas 2019. For Zeny Egoy, the woman we're meeting with here, a water connection is not a gift. It's an investment she's making in her family's future.

Meeting a WaterCredit borrower named Janine Bautista in the Philippines. Janine told us the incredible story of how she's lifting her family out of poverty, one investment at a time.

Kids playing at a water pump in Ethiopia. There's nothing like the simple joy of water.

for both families and societies. One of the greatest humanitarian tragedies of the past decade has been the war in Syria. One of its underlying causes was a long drought.[11] Over the course of four years, it decimated Syrian farmland, killing 80 percent of the country's cattle.[12] Farmers fled en masse to the cities—where they struggled to find work. As one expert explained, because of this migration, "you had a lot of angry, unemployed men helping to trigger a revolution."[13] Of course, the consequences were not confined to Syria. Refugees flooded into Europe, helping spark nationalist movements and political disruption in countries across the continent. Now imagine if we had waves of forced migration rippling around the world, with hundreds of millions of impoverished people needing not only water but jobs and homes—and imagine their desperation if all of that is in short supply. The UN estimates that by 2030 a lack of access to water could displace up to 700 million people. It would be a global refugee crisis unlike any the world has ever seen.[14]

But it's not inevitable. If more parts of the world have functioning water systems, then we can adapt these water systems when crises strike—just like we do in the United States. Investing in access today builds resilience for tomorrow.

I didn't think the world needed more reasons to expand people's access to water, but now there's another: it will help people adapt to climate change in some of the hardest-hit places.

And this message, it seems, is getting across. In 2000, when the countries of the world agreed to the Millennium Development Goals, none of the high-level goals focused on water and sanitation. In 2015, when the UN defined its agenda—the Sustainable Development Goals—for the next fifteen years, one of the principal goals (SDG 6, if you're keeping track at home) was to ensure that all people have access to water and sanitation. That same year, the World Economic Forum named water crises—that's *crises*, plural, including water shortages as well as the current lack of access—as the biggest threat of the next decade.[15]

And recently, a group of global companies—Microsoft, Dow, AB InBev and others—came together to form the Water Resilience Coalition, which is making the business case for solving this crisis. These companies see the danger—to the global economy and to their own bottom line—if the WEF's projections are right and water-related losses from climate change cause the GDP in some regions to shrink by up to 6 percent by midcentury.[16] The coalition has committed to improve the water supply through their own operations, and to work together to heighten the world's ability to withstand shocks to the supply.[17]

By the second half of the 2010s, the people who controlled the world's capital had started giving the water issue the attention it deserved. And they were more open than ever to making investments that could transform lives. This, we realized, was our shot.

◊

People are often happy to give money to nonprofits, but rarely, if ever, do they ask a nonprofit to manage their money. It's not our skill set. But in a very real sense, that was what Matt and I were inviting people to do. If we were going to raise serious capital, we needed to prove that we knew water and sanitation investments better than anyone, that we'd make the best possible use of every dollar, that we could deliver meaningful returns. In other words, we needed people to believe everything that they have been conditioned not to believe about nonprofits.

We had an extraordinary team leading our impact investing efforts: John Moyer, Alix Lebec, Hannah Kovich, and Gina Zanolli. But even they couldn't do the impossible. Why shove our square nonprofit peg into a round hole, we wondered, when there might be a better way altogether? What if we created a separate organization entirely, with a different look and feel than Water.org, and a different area of expertise? With that idea in mind, we decided to build an asset manager—our own version of, say, Fidelity or Berkshire Hathaway, the kind of organization you might trust to invest your retirement savings with. Except in our case, we wouldn't be investing in tech or health care companies—we'd be investing exclusively in expanding access to clean water and sanitation. So in 2017, we launched Water-Equity, the first asset manager dedicated to solving the global water crisis. Given that people don't usually ask movie actors or engineers to invest their money, we recruited a team of actual experts in finance to do it, led by Paul O'Connell, an old pro in asset management.

Of course—forgive me for stating the obvious—you can't run an investment group like a nonprofit. Not even this kind of investment group. About two-thirds of impact investors are called double bottom line investors—meaning that while they look for investments that do good in the world, they also want these investments to earn them the same kind of returns they could get if their money was invested in the regular market.[18] If we wanted them to invest in WASH, we couldn't tell them, "Your returns will be low, but it's for a good cause." We had to find a way to get higher returns.

The easiest and most obvious way was off-limits—indeed, totally unacceptable—to us: we did not want to drive up interest rates for household borrowers. That would increase returns, all right, but it could put people deeper in poverty. So we needed to figure out another way.

Because what we and our MFI partners were doing was new, we were convinced we could get more efficient in our operations, driving down the costs of administering the loans and driving up returns for investors. We also started to learn about something called blended finance. Which sounds like the world's most boring smoothie. But actually—please trust me on this— it's really exciting, because it offers a way for more investors to profit without making that profit on the backs of people in poverty.

With blended finance, you bring together a wide range of investors—from those with a low tolerance for risk to others with a high tolerance, from people expecting no return to people expecting a near market-rate return—and pool their resources together in the same fund. I'll spare you the details about how this works, because the important thing is that it *does* work. In fact, it works really, really well. Especially when you're launching a new type of impact investment that will meet a critical need for people in poverty.

I mentioned how difficult it was to raise our first $10 million fund. Well, for WaterEquity's second fund, Bank of America agreed to kick us off with a $5 million investment—and said they'd be happy to forgo collecting interest on that money. That act of generosity allowed investors in the fund to receive a higher return. Our first fund had targeted a 2 percent return. With Bank of America's backing, we were able to target a 3.5 percent return for our second fund. That opened us up to a whole new pool of investors. So many more investors, in fact, that our second fund was five times larger than our first. That is the power of blended finance.

With a fund that large, WaterEquity could expand its reach beyond India, to Indonesia, Cambodia, and the Philippines. We projected that as the money was deployed over the course of seven years, it would reach 4.6 million people with safe water or sanitation.

As exciting as funds like this are, we know that even at an immense scale, Water.org and WaterEquity will not be able to wrangle all the capital needed to solve this crisis. Our long-term goal is to spur *system change*—to build an enduring capital market that will connect those who need safe water with those who have the capital to fund it, so both can benefit. Of course, markets work best when value is created for both parties. We see markets working to get people water and sanitation in many places around the world, and we're pretty far along in cracking the code to make them work everywhere.

That's why we think of ourselves as social entrepreneurs. Typically, entrepreneurs find a niche, build their intellectual property, create value, and eventually go public. As *social* entrepreneurs, we are cut from the same cloth—but when we talk about going public, it means we share the IP with the world, go open source with the code, and actually advocate for other investors to learn from it, so they can become part of the enduring change we envision.

While WaterEquity was getting off the ground, we got good news at Water.org from what seemed, at first, an unlikely source: a beer company. Our team had learned that Stella Artois was interested in tackling the water crisis, so we persuaded them to launch a partnership. Stella Artois would take a portion of the profits from every beer they sold and donate it to Water.org. They would also set their marketing machine loose on the issue. This is a company that is known for great, smart, effective ads, and Matt and I were thrilled to get their team engaged in producing ad campaigns about the need for clean water—and what consumers could do about it. "Buy a Lady a Drink" was one of those campaigns, which I know sounds like something out of the fifties. But the tagline aimed to get people's attention—and it did. Once they were listening, the campaign informed them that there were millions of women in the world losing hours of their days in the search for water, and that by buying a Stella, you could help pay for water connections. "Pour It Forward" was another great campaign. Stella created special-edition versions of their famous chalices, designed by artists from the countries where Water.org works, that raised even more money to combat the water crisis. The campaign was so successful that Stella started releasing a new set of chalices each year.

For Stella, this wasn't just charity. Giving away a portion of every sale actually made financial sense. The people at Stella and their parent company, AB InBev, recognized that when people buy a beer, they're buying a little bit of refreshment, a little bit of ease—and they might want to pass on a similar feeling to the people who needed it most. If people could do some good by buying a Stella, they figured, they'd want to buy more of them. Data confirm this. Two-thirds of customers, according to a recent survey, are willing to pay a premium for products and services with a positive impact.[19]

It's not often that an NGO and a beer company find themselves in a win-win scenario, but this has been one of them. For Water.org, the partnership has not only given us much-needed funding, but it's gotten our message out. One year, Stella ran a Super Bowl ad for the #PourItForward campaign. It was designed, of course, to get people to buy beer. But it also gave Matt a chance to talk to a hundred million people about the water crisis. Matt is used to audiences that size, but there's not a chance that our organization alone could ever have made that happen.

More people were getting to know us and our work. More important, they were getting to know the issue and the fact that something could be done—was being done—about it. Better still, they wanted to be part of the solution. Their donations fueled even more growth, allowing us to help more people in more countries. Corporations like Inditex, Ecolab, and Reckitt, as well as the Target Foundation, partnered with us, putting even more wind at our back.

The private sector was getting on board, investors were signing up, and Water.org and our WaterEquity team started building on each other. Water.org's efforts showed us where funding was most urgently needed and helped build the investment pipeline—and WaterEquity gave us the power to raise that money and direct it where it needed to go.

I remember that when we first started WaterCredit, we hosted an event in India, bringing together leaders of water NGOs to talk about our idea. Just a small group showed up. The only place we could find for the meeting was a classroom where the chairs and desks were all too small for us. So they jammed themselves into the seats and tried to pay attention as I described our approach. But ten years later, by the mid-2010s, we would get more than a hundred people at sessions like these and had to rent out big rooms in hotels to meet with all the people interested in working with us. This was just one tangible sign that our reach was growing.

Our most important realization about the water crisis—the

realization that inspired all the rest—was that it was fundamentally a money problem: we needed an almost unimaginable
and seemingly unattainable amount of money in order to solve
it. But with these new systems in place, and boundless opportunities for them to keep growing, that funding problem started
to look surmountable after all.

One thing we had to figure out during this period was how to
convey the *true* return on investment for these funds. Financial returns are straightforward: numbers on a chart. Beyond
that, we'd describe our impact by counting the number of people who, thanks to the fund, had gained water and sanitation.
But even these numbers couldn't convey the actual impact that
a water connection had on people's lives. So we supplemented
our data with stories—telling our investors about people like
Boddamma, a woman whom a colleague of mine met on a trip
to India in July 2014.

When they met, Boddamma was thirty-nine. She lived with
her husband and their three teenage children—two daughters
and a son—in a slum in southern India. She worked as a daily
wage laborer, and her husband worked as a carpenter.

Water was a constant problem for the family. They lived in a
small home at the top of a steep hill, so every day, Boddamma
or one of her daughters would walk for an hour to get the heavy
pots of water and then carry them up the hill. Because the
climb was so difficult, they did as much washing and cleaning

as possible at the bottom of the hill—then carried what remained up to the house. Boddamma and her two daughters rotated staying home from work or school in order to get it all done. This meant that Boddamma lost two days of wages and her daughters each missed two days of school every week. Unsurprisingly, both girls' performance in school suffered—as did the family's economic fate.

In 2014, Boddamma decided to fix this. She took out a water loan for $167, and her local water utility installed a tap outside their door. Boddamma paid back the loan at a rate of about $15 a month—which was no trouble at all, because just the eight extra days of work she gained each month earned her *twice* the cost of the loan. And after she paid back the loan in full, Boddamma had only a small utility bill to pay.

As a result, Boddamma's daughters got to attend school every day, not just part of the week—and were learning so much more as a result. One of the girls said: "I don't want others to suffer like I suffered." To help their neighbors, the family started sharing their water with three other families—an additional eleven people—for free.

Just think about the ripple effects of that single $167 loan. A woman is now able to earn the money she needs to take care of her family. Two girls are now able to dedicate their time to their education—and to focus on becoming whatever they want to be in life. And eleven more neighbors get the benefits—in time and money and good health—of a nearby water source. Think of all that good, from just a single loan. Now imagine it multiplied by millions.

When we went to Davos in 2019, the airline lost Matt's suitcase. If Bono thought Matt's sweater vest was embarrassing five years earlier, I can't imagine how Matt felt about having to borrow my clothes. (Still, "Who Wore It Better?" is not a contest I'm ever going to win against Matt Damon.) You could tell, though, that even in my unfashionable sweater, Matt was feeling far more at ease this time as we walked around in the cold, making our case to anyone who would listen. I know I was. We knew from the beginning that the best way to attract support was to run up numbers no one could ignore. And by now, we had those numbers.

By 2019, we were able to say we'd mobilized more than *$1 billion* to fight the water crisis. That didn't mean we'd received $1 billion in donations and investment dollars—that kind of capital still remains a dream for us. It meant that through the cycle of lending we'd set in motion, our partners had distributed more than a billion dollars' worth of loans. (Today, that number stands at over *$3 billion*.) Because we've scaled so quickly and efficiently, thanks in large part to our incredible chief insights officer, Rich Thorsten, and chief operating officer, Vedika Bhandarkar, every dollar we've invested across our organization has created, in turn, thirteen dollars' worth of impact. That's leverage. Even among the richest folks on the planet, the word *billion* gets attention. Many of the people who've succeeded to that degree are problem solvers at their core. They want to put their money behind things that really work. With these kinds of numbers, we had proof that this wasn't just a nice idea, but a real solution—something that could go a long way toward solving this crisis.

So the investment world started taking us more seriously. I remember when we first went to Davos, we appeared on the CNBC business news show *Squawk Box*. We were presented back then as a curiosity in the business world, a novelty. Then, in the years that followed, when we went back on the show, we had actual investment funds to talk about, and actual performance metrics to tout. By 2019, we were invited onto the show along with major players in the business world like Carlos Brito and Anne Finucane.

Once we had gotten this kind of validation, more and more funders agreed to invest. In the same amount of time it took us to raise $10 million for our first fund, we raised the $50 million for our second. To date, both funds are on track to reach just as many people as expected. So we set our sights higher still: we raised a $150 million fund. Funding on that scale allows us to reach substantially more people—and quickly.

Between Matt's previous organization and my own, it took us twenty years to reach a million people. By 2019, between Water.org, WaterEquity, and all our partners across the world, we were reaching *2* million people *every quarter*.

8

VENTURE
PHILANTHROPY

POV: Matt Damon

If this was a movie script, we'd now confront what we call a pacing issue.

At this point in our story, obstacles have been overcome, momentum is building, goals that once appeared impossible are now within reach. We seem to be moving swiftly toward the climactic scene—when Gary stands up at a podium at, I don't know, the United Nations and declares that the global water crisis . . . is over.

But life doesn't always unfold the way you'd want to script it. Suddenly, our climactic scene was deferred. Our plot development went to hell and sent us scrambling for a rewrite.

We had no warning things would take this turn. We started

out the year 2019 feeling great. WaterCredit programs were thriving. WaterEquity fundraising was going better than ever. I was wearing Gary's clothes at Davos and finding they fit pretty well. Then something strange started happening: the donation dollars that Water.org relies on didn't grow like we were expecting them to. Instead, they went *down*—by almost 20 percent.

Twenty percent is not a rounding error. Cut something, cut anything, 20 percent and you're going to feel it. As you'd expect, Gary and the team mobilized to figure out what was causing this. It wasn't because our projects were failing to hit their targets—in fact, they were often exceeding their targets. The decline in funding, it was clear, had nothing to do with our performance at all. Or anything else you could point to, add up, put your finger on.

It turned out the issue was one that lots of other NGOs and social enterprises had faced at some point in their life cycle: the whims of philanthropy. It sounds crazy—it is crazy!—but philanthropy, like fashion, like music, has vogues. One minute you're in, then something new comes along . . . and if you're not quite out, well, you're not as in as you used to be. As Gary described, water was in vogue during the Water Decade of the 1980s, then fell out of vogue. (When people name a decade after you, that's a pretty good indication you're in vogue.) Causes come and go—remember the Ice Bucket Challenge to address ALS?— even though the issues remain. And by 2019, some of our key donors had their heads turned by other, newer funding opportunities, so they stopped funding us and started funding those.

Again, to be honest, we were totally unprepared for this. We should have remembered the Water Decade and its unceremonious end. Maybe we just thought that things were different this time. I mean, we'd been doing the work—building momentum, running up the numbers, winning converts and gaining investors, testing and improving a model that just plain worked, and beautifully. We'd built an incredibly efficient engine that ran like a dream: give it a little fuel, and it would go and go. But suddenly we were low on gas.

It was hard to shake the feeling that I was doing something wrong. Or maybe just not doing enough of the right things. I knew our fundamentals were strong and our team was incredible. I was well aware that I had the easy job—to get more people to pay attention to that good work and to support it. And I felt like I was failing.

The same year our funding started going down, Gary went to the Skoll World Forum conference in Oxford, a gathering where social entrepreneurs talk about their projects and their plans. These were some of the most creative social entrepreneurs on the planet—people working to get girls into schools, fight human trafficking, improve global health. This kind of event always gets Gary energized—he comes back buzzing with stories to tell and ideas to try. But this time, the social entrepreneurs hadn't talked much about their innovations. The mood was downbeat.

What they talked about was *money*—or the lack of it. Like Water.org, nearly all of them were having a hard time getting funding. Here were leaders of social enterprises with incredibly high potential to succeed, yet many of them were having trouble keeping the lights on. They were at the Skoll conference because they'd already demonstrated they had well-established, wildly successful ideas—ideas that were ready to scale even further. Still, no one would give these entrepreneurs the capital to grow.

This was completely at odds with what Gary and I had seen in the for-profit investment world. Investors tend to bet big on big ideas—especially big, successful ideas. In the world of venture capital, the better you are at solving a big challenge, the larger an investment you tend to get. That's how venture capital helps great ideas to generate a greater impact—and, not incidentally, greater returns.

But there weren't enough donors, it seemed, who were ready to apply that way of thinking to social enterprises. When donations are based on whims and vogues instead of performance, great organizations see their funding dry up. Gary and I worried we were heading that way.

And this, of course, wasn't the only threat to our hopes and plans. For every one of us who was around in 2020, that year will serve as a watershed moment for the rest of our lives, the line of division between before and after, the time when it became painfully clear how little we can take for granted.

I'll never forget when everything stopped. In March,

Water.org's offices, like offices and restaurants and schools and everything everywhere in the world, were closed up as COVID-19 forced us into our respective bubbles. Me, I was lucky. I had been shooting a movie in a seaside village in Ireland. It was a beautiful, peaceful place—a contrast to the chaos consuming the world. My family and I stayed put.

From the vantage point of the village, watching the pandemic spread across the world was eerie, in part because I'd rehearsed for it—literally. A decade earlier, I'd made a movie called *Contagion*, a title that gets right to the point: a deadly respiratory disease overwhelms the planet. The real-life horror story that played out in 2020 had, therefore, a familiar story arc: the slow initial response; the widespread panic; the chilling quiet of mass quarantines; the phony leaders selling phony cures; and, of course, the insistent reminder: *wash your hands*.

But again, this was real life, as much as it seemed like dystopian fiction. And as I stood there at the sink at the house, singing two rounds of "Happy Birthday" to be sure I'd washed my hands long enough, I'd think about the hundreds of millions of people who couldn't do that, because they had no access to water. Around that time, one reporter calculated how many times a day people found themselves in situations where public health officials advised them to wash their hands—after touching a surface outside the home, for example, or after coughing or sneezing—and it added up to ten or more times a day. For a family of four to do that much handwashing would take more than twenty gallons of water a day.[1]

Obviously, that's not an option for people who have to carry all that water (plus the additional water they need for every other purpose) in cans or buckets—people who have to treat every drop like the scarce resource it is. And of course, following public safety orders to stay at home to avoid catching or spreading the virus is impossible if your home has no water or sanitation—which means you're stuck in a deadly Catch-22.

And not just homes: hospitals! Here's a shocking fact. In low-income countries, a quarter of health care facilities lack soap and running water.[2] In other words, in the middle of a global pandemic, health care workers don't have the water they need to wash their hands. It's beyond belief. The world was focused, reasonably enough, on increasing the supply of PPE—personal protective equipment. Well, water is the most basic, most valuable PPE there is.

Suddenly access to water and sanitation had become, even more than before, a life-or-death issue. But Water.org and our partners were totally hamstrung. The pandemic essentially shut down our efforts to increase the number of water connections. As we've described, that work happens face-to-face, as loan officers go from one house to the next in poor communities, providing in-person trainings and transactions. You can't do that on Zoom. So for a while, we couldn't do it at all.

And as the movement of people around the world slowed to a halt, so did the movement of money. The economic consequences of the pandemic rippled across the planet; and for us, the consequence was that donations slowed even further. Soon after the start of the pandemic, Water.org's largest donor notified us that they wouldn't be able to provide their scheduled support—which added up to a third of our budget.

For years, we'd been talking about how much bigger we could grow, how many more people we could reach. All of a sudden, like many organizations, we were scrambling to figure out how to survive the next few months. The goal of ending the crisis—which had felt for years like it was getting closer—suddenly seemed further away.

When vogues and sudden crises can throw us off course, how can we keep our focus? How can we make steady progress against a problem that won't yield to anything short of our full attention and full dedication?

There's no easy answer to that. But part of the answer, without doubt, is that whatever challenges get thrown our way, we have to keep reminding people that water is central to addressing nearly all of them. Even to stopping them before they start.

Take health crises, for example. Water and sanitation, as I've described, are essential to stopping the spread of viruses like COVID-19. Next time—and I'm sorry, but scientists are telling us there probably will be a next time—they can help us prepare before the pandemic hits.[3]

To help explain how, let me describe the ending of *Contagion*. So spoiler alert, I guess—if it still counts as a spoiler when we've all lived through the real-life version.

At the end of the movie, the camera cuts away from the characters we've come to know, and suddenly, you're looking at a bat. The bat lives in a forest, but the trees are being bull-dozed to make room for farmland. So the bat takes refuge in an industrial pig farm, where it drops a piece of banana it was eating. The pig that eats the banana is later cooked in a Hong Kong restaurant—by a chef who doesn't wash up before shaking hands with Gwyneth Paltrow, my wife in the movie. She becomes, in this way, patient zero, as a new deadly virus passes from bat to pig to human.

I mention all this because experts pretty much agree that the three factors you see in that scene—destruction of natural habitats, which brings wild animals into proximity with humans; industrial agriculture, which weakens animals' immune systems; and globalization, which puts all humans in closer contact with one another—create the conditions for new diseases to spread.

I think a lot of us, at some point during the COVID-19 pandemic, said: "We should have known this would happen!" Well, that's still true when it comes to the next one. Dr. Simon Reid, a researcher in communicable diseases, put it like this: "If you don't resolve the conditions that generated the problem, then we sit waiting for the next probability equation to come through. And it will."[4]

And here's another thing that *Contagion*'s screenwriter, Scott Z. Burns, got right: handwashing is always going to be our first defense against a health crisis. When Scott sent me the script for the movie, he attached a note that said "Read this and then go wash your hands."[5]

Universal water and sanitation access will make pandemics less likely to begin in the first place—and slower to spread if they do. As COVID ran its course, this message started to break through. *The Washington Post* ran a powerful story under the headline "Living Through a Pandemic When Your Access to Water Is Difficult"; *The New York Times* asked "How Do You Fight the Coronavirus Without Running Water?"[6, 7] (The answer: not very effectively.) Gary and I were invited to discuss the issue on the TIME 100 Talks program. We knew we didn't have to convince a US audience that clean water could help stop the spread of the virus—people already got that. Gary and I just tried to drive the point home.

Of course, people who lacked access to water understood this, too, on an even deeper level. That's why, despite the obstacles to outreach, demand for water and sanitation loans in some places actually grew in 2020—so much so that in the biggest country where we work, India, we *exceeded* our impact targets for the year. And we all came together, with our friends and family, to keep Water.org working. Thanks to large and small donations from many, and hard work and innovation by all, we were able to keep moving forward, keep doing the work on the ground.

We've emerged more urgently committed to our mission than ever. The pandemic made painfully clear that what happens on the other side of the world can affect a family in your hometown. Access to clean water and sanitation is going to make these communities—and therefore all of us, in a world where disease cannot be confined by borders—a lot safer and better able to handle what's next.

We've been saying for years that people's lives depend on getting safe water and sanitation. Now, it's clear that *our* lives depend on it, too.

That's even more obvious when you think about the other crisis that will dominate the world's attention in the coming decades: climate change.

Gary explained how universal water and sanitation are crucial if we're ever going to adapt to climate change—access makes vulnerable people more resilient. Adaptation is essential, but it can't be our only approach; we can't afford to accept that life on Earth is going to be scarier and deadlier, that wildfires and hurricanes and famines are our fate from here forward, and all that we can do is adapt. We also need to be doing everything in our power to stop climate change, to mitigate it.

And here, too, water can make a difference. Water and sanitation systems that are bad for *people's* health are also bad for the *planet's* health. Human waste, for example, releases methane—a greenhouse gas with a warming effect at least *28 times stronger* than CO_2.[8] Which means that globally, waste and wastewater generate more greenhouse gases each year than *all the cars in the United States*.[9, 10] Think how much focus we put on making vehicles greener—the battles over new fuel standards, the electric cars vying to be the next big thing. But human waste—well, it's never going to attract more attention than the newest Tesla. If you ever see "human waste" trending on Twitter, something very bad has happened.

Still, unpleasant as it is, we do need to spend more time thinking about it, or at least dealing with it. Globally, 80 percent of wastewater goes untreated.[11] As a result, waste gets into the water supply, making people sick, and releases more methane, making the planet sick.

There's another kind of waste we need to care more about: the energy we waste in moving water from one place to another. People in poverty might be getting water—they wouldn't be alive if they weren't—but they're getting it extremely inefficiently. In many rural communities, the energy people are wasting is their own labor, which has minimal environmental impact. But in denser places, inefficient water systems consume massive amounts of dirty energy. Water utilities use an incredible amount of electricity to pump water from faraway sources because nearby sources are too polluted. On top of that, utilities use a lot of diesel fuel to power the tanker trucks that drive water around. And they waste much of that energy by losing massive quantities of water.

In 2019, Gary and I went to the Philippines and visited with officials at a utility there. Manila Water, the country's biggest water utility, uses enough electricity annually to power 21,000 American homes for a year.[12, 13] Officials at Laguna Water, a joint venture between the provincial government and

Manila Water, told us that ten years earlier, they had been losing 48 percent of their water supply due to leaky pipes. In other words, in a country where millions of people lack clean water, nearly half of Laguna Water's water supply—and thus half the energy they use to pump it—was being wasted.

The utility has really turned things around: the amount of wasted water is down to 21 percent—still a lot, but a big improvement. They've been investing in infrastructure—replacing water mains, repairing leaks, improving their distribution system. But this success story is all too rare. Utilities in developing countries lose, on average, 35 percent of their water to leaks. That waste is part of the reason why water is so expensive in some of the world's poorest communities.[14] And if we don't fix these systems, the problem's going to get much worse as the world continues to urbanize. To serve even more people, cities will have to bring in even more water, which will take even more energy. Finding new water sources is also energy intensive.

But again, there's a different path—we just have to take it. Laguna Water has shown us the way: fix your infrastructure, waste less water, waste less energy. Others are designing smarter water and sanitation systems, which run on less energy and reduce the pollution from wastewater at the same time.

I know it's tough to get anyone except Gary White excited about improving wastewater treatment. Unless you're Bill Gates, who has been known to bring a jar of poop with him to big talks.[15] (If you're not Bill Gates, this will clear a room pretty quickly.) But there's good reason to get excited about it.

I mentioned that treating wastewater can keep greenhouse gases out of the atmosphere. Well, incredibly, this waste can also be a source of energy *itself,* generating the very power we need to move our water and treat our sanitation. Globally, human waste converted to fuel could have a value equivalent to about $9.5 billion worth of natural gas.[16]

As UNESCO Director-General Audrey Azoulay put it, "Water does not need to be a problem—it can be part of the solution."[17] Water can definitely be a part of the solution when it comes to climate change, to health crises, to inequality. Johan Rock-ström, who runs the Resilience Centre at Stockholm University, put it this way: "Water is the bloodstream of the biosphere and the determinant of our future."[18] That's scientist-speak for that old Thales quote I mentioned: "Water is the first principle of everything."

If we keep spreading that message so that people every-where embrace it, we can change the way we think about water—not as a cause whose time had come and gone, not as a second- or third-tier concern, but as a solution. As an opportunity, in more ways than we can possibly measure.

◊

Fifty years ago, John D. Rockefeller III coined a term he believed would describe a different kind of giving: *venture philan-thropy.* His hope, he said, was to start a new and "adventurous approach to funding unpopular social causes."[19]

Venture philanthropy, as Rockefeller defined it, doesn't follow the whims of donors or the trends of the moment. Instead, it's distributed more like venture capital: funding goes to the most promising ideas that need capital in order to fulfill their promise. It comes with few strings attached because progress depends on taking risks. And as an idea succeeds, its funding grows—allowing it to scale to the point where "changing the world" isn't just hype.

Venture philanthropy never quite took off during Rockefeller's lifetime. But venture philanthropy's time has come. It's no secret that the concentration of wealth is at an all-time high. That's not something to celebrate, even if you've had good luck and have done well financially, as I have. None of us should be satisfied with a system that is this unjust, this inequitable. The world's billionaires alone hold as much wealth as 60 percent of the world's population. That means the richest 2,153 people hold more wealth than *4.6 billion* people combined.[20]

But one bright spot, just possibly, is that a growing number of those 2,153 individuals have been committing themselves publicly to putting their wealth to work on behalf of the broader good. That's the idea behind The Giving Pledge, the movement started by Bill Gates, Melinda French Gates, and Warren Buffett that has inspired hundreds of billionaires to pledge to give away at least half their wealth.

Most of these folks earned their billions in business—which means they're familiar, many of them, with venture capital and have an entrepreneurial mindset. So as big philanthropy grows bigger, groups like this could start functioning more like VCs, searching out potentially game-changing ideas and giving them the funding they need to prove their concept and to scale.

We've seen some early signs this is starting to happen. Andy Peykoff, who founded Niagara Bottling, has provided millions in big bets on WaterCredit and WaterEquity. Even when those ideas were still unproven, he saw potential and took a risk on us. And he's still doing it today: recently, he committed an additional $5 million for us to hire the team to bring the next WaterEquity fund to life.

Maybe, just maybe, we'll start to see more big bets like this. In 2018, Gary was invited to make a presentation at The Giving Pledge's annual gathering. The group gets together every year to educate donors on pressing global issues. To help members determine how to make the biggest impact with their money, the group highlights a few promising areas for investment. Water had never been on the list—until that year.

Gary saw a lot of interest in our model: follow-up questions, breakout discussions. Some of those conversations are ongoing. But so far, all these discussions have resulted in just a single donation. This reflects the larger problem of vast (I mean, the word *vast* barely begins to describe it) sums of money sitting idle, even after that money has been pledged. Right now, of all the wealth that has been put into foundations, a staggering 95 percent is locked away in sheltered accounts—which give big tax benefits to donors but fail to serve any social purpose.

And look—I understand this is difficult. Figuring out where

you and your money can have the greatest impact, selecting which issues will get your attention and which issues won't, can be a complicated process, and it can be an emotional one. If not for Bono's prodding, I'm sure I would have taken a lot longer to sort out my own thinking.

But Gary and I are hopeful that the billionaires will get bolder and move faster, as MacKenzie Scott and Jack Dorsey have recently started to do—understanding that each day of delay will be, for many millions of people, another day lost to disease and deprivation.

Ultimately, though, these big new donors are not the only ones with the power to take an "entrepreneurial approach" to improving our world. We can all do that. Even if you've only got a small sum to put in, you can play a role in giving potentially transformative ideas the chance to prove themselves. Donations of any size are a vote of confidence in a social enterprise—a boost to its ability to innovate, create change, and get results.

There were times in recent years when we felt weighed down by the challenges of the moment. But if we widen the frame a bit, beyond the daily hurdles and depressing headlines, we can see that momentum continues to build.

When we started work on this book in 2018, I wrote: "Water.org has reached 22 million people." Before we were done writing, it was 25 million. Then 30. Just before this book went to print, we updated the number again—to 40 million. By the time you read this, even that number will be out of date.

When I start from the perspective of where we've been— when I think about those first projects I did in the Sahara Desert, when getting clean water for even one community was a victory—the number of people we've reached is staggering. But when I think about it from a different perspective—not how far we've come, but how far we've yet to go—the numbers don't look quite as incredible. They feel like a start. Remember, there are still 785 million people in the world who lack access to safe water, and 2 billion who lack adequate sanitation.

So for us, the most exciting thing isn't the number of people we've reached. It's the systems change that had to happen— and did—in order to see that kind of progress. The increase was only possible because world leaders committed to ending the water crisis. Because people around the world put their money where their values are. Because investors started seeking returns that aren't just measured in dollars. And most of all, because millions of incredibly resourceful and brave people took out a microloan, paid it back in full, and took charge of their own future.

We knew from the beginning that to solve this crisis, we'd need a global movement. And when I look at the whole arc of this story, and the incredible progress we've seen over the past three decades, I can see that it's possible. In fact, it may already be happening.

9

THE WAVE

POV: Gary White

We've tried to avoid water metaphors in this book.

I'll be honest. It hasn't been easy. *Testing the waters. Come hell or high water.* There's a million more where those came from. A flood, if you will, of on-brand clichés.

But we're nearing the end here, and before we wrap up I'm giving myself license to use one, and only one, water metaphor:

To end the crisis, we need a wave.

What's interesting about waves is where they get their power.

When you're standing on the beach, watching the waves crash in—watching them build, move, and break—you'd never know that their energy, their momentum, comes from water molecules spanning many miles of sea, working together in unseen ways, lifting when it was their moment to rise.

During the Water Decade, there were people with a lot of power—government leaders and development experts and multilateral organizations—pushing as hard as they could for change from the top. But they didn't do enough to harness the resources or the energy or the capability of the people their programs were trying to help. So after all that buildup, the wave never materialized.

What we're seeing now is very different. What we're seeing is what can happen—what incredible things can happen—when you enlist the skills and smarts and financial power of many millions of people, from the bottom of the economic pyramid up, as well as from the top down. People in poverty are seeing the possibility of change—the reality of change, in so many places—and they're ready to be part of it.

The wave is reaching them, and it's their moment to rise.

For the 40 million people who now have the access they need, thanks to WaterCredit, this has already happened. But again, there are still billions of people out there left to reach.

So how can we reach them?

You might find it useful—we definitely do—to look at these billions in roughly three categories, with each group more difficult to reach than the last.

By now, you know a lot about the first group. They're the

focus of this book. They're the people who are willing and able to solve their water and sanitation problems—if someone will give them a small loan to get started. As you've read, it's taken time to demonstrate that this group can be part of their own solution. But over the past ten years, we, and they, have shown that they can. We project that there are about 500 million people like them. When we have enough resources, we'll be able to reach them really quickly.

There's a lot more work to do on this front. Half a billion people is, well, a lot of people! But the fact that this approach is succeeding, that it's building such momentum, has given us license to think even bigger. We've started to focus on the next group that lacks access to water and sanitation: people for whom microloans alone aren't going to be enough.

That's because where this group lives, something essential is missing: infrastructure. In parts of many cities, and especially in the perimeter just outside urban areas, there are no pipes carrying water under the streets; there is no sewage system; there's nothing to tap into.

This group, right now, is literally beyond the reach of water utilities.

So why, then, don't the utilities just extend into these areas? The need is there. The population is there. And with the benefit of microloans, the paying customers are there.

But most utilities don't see poor people as customers just yet. As we've described, that's a new mindset, and it hasn't taken hold everywhere. The way many utilities see it, every additional customer makes them lose more money.

And utilities have enough trouble providing service and covering costs as it is. Governments often force them to ratchet down the price they charge so that constituents—voters—can get water that's pretty much free. Which sounds great, except for the fact that when prices get too low, utilities can't make enough money to keep supplies flowing, or keep water clean, or repair leaking pipes. These inefficient systems waste energy and water, as Matt described, and they emit greenhouse gases. They also leave hundreds of millions of people without water and sanitation.

So this is the next hurdle—the next mountain we've got to summit. And it's getting steeper. Since 2000, every single day an average of 16,500 people have moved to urban slums in search of work. That's 6 million people every year.[1] They need water, obviously. They need sanitation. They need utilities that work and water systems that extend to where the population is living and growing.

Fortunately, a lot of smart people at the UN and the World Bank and other organizations are on the case. They're working with utilities to help them become more efficient—and better funded. The picture is already improving in places, as we saw in the Philippines. Countries like Cambodia, Peru, and others are figuring out how to expand their water and sanitation systems.

Water.org is stepping up its support, too. We're working with utilities in Indonesia, for example; we're letting them know that if they expand service to a given area, paying customers live there and will connect. We're so confident of this that we're facilitating loan guarantees to utilities, giving them a chance to get the capital to expand the infrastructure where it's most needed. It's working well.

Once Water.org has helped utilities improve operations and find new paying customers, WaterEquity can fund desperately needed improvements to their infrastructure—laying new pipes, fixing leaks, building wastewater treatment plants. Funding these improvements could help millions of people get access to water and sanitation, keep massive amounts of methane and CO_2 out of our atmosphere, and show the world that water and sanitation utilities can be a smart investment. The idea is that WaterEquity can be the pioneers of new water utility investments, the ones who map the territory and show global capital markets that utilities paired with a known customer base are a smart bet. Once we do that, other investors will follow our lead.

Our goal is to make sure that everyone on the planet who wants to invest in water and sanitation has the chance to do so—at a fair price.

At that point, we'll have one group left to reach: people who simply can't pay for the water and sanitation solutions they need. In some rural communities, poverty is just so extreme that loans aren't a real option. To make matters worse, these areas are so remote, so far off the grid, that the slow expansion of water utilities isn't going to reach them any time soon. Getting household access to water service there is a hugely expensive proposition. Extreme costs, extreme poverty—that's a dire combination. To help this group get access, communal wells and water systems will need to be heavily subsidized. Governments of these low-income countries will be the primary drivers of these projects, with support from wealthy nations and from NGOs that reach the poorest, most rural regions— the final frontier of the global water crisis.

For all the reasons we've described, charity-led water projects were never going to be effective as a first solution—let alone the only solution. But once the world has reached the other two groups with market-based solutions, the scale of the problem will, at long last, be reduced enough that we can muster the resources to fix what remains of it. And we'll finally be able to end the crisis for good.

A little more than a decade ago, when my dad, Jerry White, was nearing the end of his life, he told me something that I almost couldn't believe.

We were driving through Kansas City. Like many men of his generation, my dad didn't tell a lot of stories about himself, so when we were afraid we'd soon be losing him, we rented a big van for the whole family and took everybody around the area where he grew up, asking him, in effect, to narrate the trip—to tell us what we didn't know about his life.

As we drove through his old neighborhood, he pointed at a house his family once rented. He told us that when he lived there, they had an outhouse in their backyard. Not only that:

when the city finally extended the sewage system to his family's street—giving them a chance, finally, at indoor plumbing—the rent went up and they could no longer afford it. In fact, they got evicted.

I couldn't believe what I was hearing. Here I was, working for years to help people halfway across the world get sanitation—completely unaware that when my dad was growing up, he hadn't even had a toilet in his own house.

Progress in this work can feel so slow. But when I hear a story like the one my father told me, it also feels *fast*. In the course of just one generation, water and sanitation can go from something you can't access or afford to something you're able to take for granted.

You can see this in lots of places, if you take the time to look. As recently as the start of the twentieth century, a large part of the population in Manhattan was living without clean water. In some neighborhoods, the water and sanitation systems had been built, but many people had no access to them. On the Lower East Side, for example, people had been living above water pipes for seventy years without a tap or a toilet inside their tenement.[2]

But then, in 1901, a law passed that gave the majority of poor New Yorkers access to water lines. Today, of course, the idea of a New York apartment without water is unthinkable.

Progress is possible. And right now, we have the power to make that progress move even faster—across a vast landscape of countries that have typically been left behind. People there are writing their own success stories—investing in their own solutions—taking control of their own fates and futures. If we keep pushing, then someday soon, a world where some have water and sanitation and some do not will be something that exists only in memory.

POV: Matt Damon

In order for any of this to happen, though, we need you. The person reading this book. Maybe it's strange to start addressing you directly, now—like you're watching a musical, and it's the very last song, and suddenly they start doing audience participation.

But the fact is that this movement can't be powered only by the people who are affected by the crisis. It also has to involve the people who aren't—the two out of three people in the world who *do* have access to sanitation, the eight in nine who *do* have access to clean water. A wave can't be sustained if the majority of the water in the sea doesn't budge.

To be honest, figuring out how to make this happen has been hard. Once, out of curiosity, I went on YouTube and searched for the video of a panel discussion Gary and I had done about the water issue. It had a hundred views. I have a very limited understanding of social media—as my kids will tell you—but even to me, a hundred seemed . . . low. Then I searched for a video that Sarah Silverman and I made back when she was dating my nemesis, Jimmy Kimmel, a song about our hooking up behind his back. I checked the views on that one: 20 million. Okay, so this was an unfair comparison. No panel discussion about water is going to go viral.

But that's kind of my point. If we wanted to cut through the noise, if we wanted to get people to really hear what we had to say about the issue, we were going to have to get more creative about it.

We've tried a lot of ways to do that over the years. As Gary mentioned, Stella Artois has been a great partner of ours, and their marketing and branding people have worked with our team to help get us out of our earnest nonprofit comfort zone. We came up with a social experiment where we told customers in restaurants and hotels that there was no running water, and they'd have to wait a few hours for a glass of water or a shower. We had hidden cameras waiting to see how they reacted. (The answer: not well.) Then, right when they were realizing what an inconvenience this was going to be for them, we rolled a video showing them that for millions of people, waiting for water is an everyday occurrence—not just waiting for it, but hauling it across great distances in heavy buckets. Our intent wasn't to show people being asses in their privilege. It was to connect them, viscerally, to what people around the world are facing. We had a feeling that when the prospect of going without water became real to people, they'd be able to imagine someone else's experience. Many of them were really moved by it. We saw a lot of tears on that project.

We also wanted to make people laugh. In the early days of Water.org, I was a little self-conscious that people were going to focus on my involvement, because they knew my name, when what was really driving the organization was Gary and his ideas. So I figured the least I could do was to make an idiot out of myself for the cause. And I've done that—many times. Very convincingly, I'm told. Like the time Ellen DeGeneres said she'd donate to Water.org if I did an obstacle course in a golf cart while wearing a sumo suit. Mission accomplished. Or the time I put on a Santa costume, beard and belly and everything, and recorded myself trying to convince kids that what they actually wanted for Christmas was not a new toy, but a Water.org-branded CamelBak water bottle. No takers.

I've also spent a lot of time talking—publicly—about toilets. Probably more time than my agent might like. The Water.org team once staged a fake press conference where I announced that I was going on strike and would refuse to go to the bathroom until the water and sanitation crisis had been resolved. I regret to report that I broke my own strike. But not before we got some familiar people to announce that they were going on strike, too: Jessica Biel, Jason Bateman, Olivia Wilde, Richard Branson, Bono. You can imagine the jokes about getting people to give a shit. One YouTuber who supported the strike said: "It's an incredibly important issue. I'm glad it's being supported in the most dumbass way possible."

You probably won't read this in the *Harvard Business Review*, but sometimes the most dumbass way is the best way. For us, it's definitely brought more attention and more donations. The video of the toilet strike announcement got almost

1.5 million views. Not quite Sarah Silverman levels, but it's a lot more than a hundred.

One sanitation expert who'd been working on the issue for years used to give presentations that included a Photoshopped picture of Angelina Jolie lounging suggestively in front of a toilet, to give sanitation the sex appeal the issue deserved. After the toilet strike, the expert swapped out the fake photo of Angelina for an actual picture of me with a toilet seat around my neck.[3] Which, to me, was a sign we were doing something right. Now I can claim that I, and not Angelina Jolie, am the face of the global toilet issue.

All these efforts to build the movement, though, share the same limitation: they buy us no more than a couple minutes of people's attention. That's enough time to explain that the crisis exists—but not enough to express, let alone explain, that we can actually end it. So we came up with a different way to tell our story. You're reading it right now.

Gary and I wrote a book because, honestly, we needed more than a couple minutes to tell you this story. We wanted you to meet, as we have, some of the people who have struggled, then triumphed, over the circumstances they were dealt. We wanted you to see the wave building—and how you can be a part of it.

So how *can* you be a part of it?

We've talked a lot about money in this book, because the

water and sanitation crisis is, at heart, more of a funding problem than, say, a technology problem. So the most direct solution is for lots more people to give what they can.

So if Gary and I have managed to convince you—and I hope we have—that what we're describing is the smartest possible solution to ending the water crisis, and if you have extra dollars to give, then I hope you'll donate. Donations are what helps Water.org reach tens of millions of people—and build water and sanitation markets that can grow and grow.

There's another way to contribute beyond dollars: you can tell the story of the crisis and how we can solve it. Talk about it; write about it; post about it. Some dismiss speaking out online as slacktivism. But telling this story, bringing that awareness to the decisions that people make in their lives—it really does matter. When people see others rising up, some will be moved to rise up, too.

The fact is, for all we've made of this wave metaphor, humans don't rise up simply because of the laws of physics. We have to make a choice. And that choice—even on its own, as an individual act—can make a difference. But we know, at the same time, that the actions of any one individual are not going to solve the water crisis. Trust me—Gary has tried!

But when we talk about our efforts, we bring other people along with us—and then they bring other people along with them—until, over time, we've created a movement far larger and more powerful than ever seemed possible. When we lend our effort and energy to something larger than ourselves—

when we see and join the rising tide—that's when we realize the power we truly possess.

◊

A world where every person has clean water and sanitation is a very different world—so different that it's kind of hard to imagine.

But here's what the data—grounded not in theory, but in experience—say we should expect. We know that when people get access to clean water, more women have the chance to earn an income and support themselves by the power of their own labor. We know that as women are empowered, many delay having children until later in life and have fewer kids overall— which leaves them better able to take care of their families. And of course, families with multiple incomes are better able to lift themselves out of poverty.

As waterborne diseases decline, fewer parents will face the unbearable tragedy of losing a child. We'll see stunting become rarer: children will grow taller and have fewer lifelong health problems; their bodies and minds will be able to develop to their fullest potential. We'll probably see bigger graduating classes—since fewer girls will have dropped out along the way to focus on getting water for their families, and fewer girls and boys will have missed school because of waterborne diseases. And as these kids grow up, we'll see what they, with the benefit of good health and an education, are able to contribute to their families, their communities, and the rest of the world.

So that's the big stuff.

But there will be other changes, too, changes that are hard to quantify but are important beyond measure. Like the safety and simple comfort of having somewhere private when you need to go to the bathroom. Or the relief of a glass of cool water after working outside in the sun. Or the security of knowing that the thing you need most in the world isn't going to leave you permanently bedridden or blind or dead. Or the sense of possibility when you can spend your days tracing different paths, pursuing different goals.

There are billions of different ways, for billions of different people, that life is going to change. Of course, there's no eye-opening stat that can convey all that. But we do have stories. I know I do.

I think of a family we met in Hyderabad, India. They'd just gotten a tap installed, and they were treating it like a shrine. I mean that literally: they were lighting candles and incense around it, circling it with flowers. That's what the water tap meant to them.

I think of a woman one of our team members met in a village outside Bangalore. The woman was wrinkled from age, but she stood tall, looking distinguished. She shared that, years ago, she and other women in her community would go for days without eating or drinking—to avoid the embarrassment and danger of having to relieve themselves in the open fields. But our colleague told us that you could hear, in the woman's voice, how proud she was that she had gotten a loan to build a toilet, and finally rid herself of the fear that used to dominate her days.

And I think of a girl I met at one of our projects in Haiti. Like so many girls, she'd been the person who collected water for her family, taking that long walk to and from the well. I asked her how old she was. Thirteen, she said—the age, at the time, of my oldest daughter.

Now that she no longer had to spend her afternoons taking that long walk to water, I asked her what she was going to do with her time. "More time to do more homework?" I said.

She looked at me in that way kids do sometimes, when they're surprised an adult could be so clueless. "No!" she said. "I'm at the top of my class." It was clear she was telling the truth.

Then she told me what she was going to do with her time, the time that a water tap had given back to her.

"I'm going to play!"

I thought again of that old phrase—"Water is life." Some interpret it to mean that we need water in order to stay alive, and of course that's true. But for so many people, a source of clean water doesn't just ensure their survival. It brings freedom. It brings joy.

It brings a chance to finally just *live*.

Acknowledgments

Writing a book is hard work. Writing one during a global pandemic, not to mention a time of social reckoning and economic upheaval—well, let's just say it was harder than I thought it would be! I couldn't have done it without the love and support of my wife, Becky, who stood shoulder to shoulder with me in my career from the very beginning. I also want to thank my amazing kids, Henry and Anna, for their support and understanding during my absences as I traveled the world to advance the mission of Water.org and WaterEquity.

My parents, Kathy and Jerry White, and particularly my mother, fully demonstrated to me what it means to live a life of service. She instilled a sense of purpose and passion that fuels me to this day. All of my siblings, siblings-in-law, and Becky's parents have been great champions of this work since the first days back in 1990.

On behalf of Matt and me, I want to give enormous thanks to

Acknowledgments

Jeff Shesol and Ellie Schaack of West Wing Writers, who gave indispensable guidance and support and expert wordsmithing throughout the writing process.

We also wish to give thanks to those who read the manuscript in advance to help us make sure our words aligned with our values: Magdalene Matthews, author and senior program officer at the Conrad N. Hilton Foundation's Safe Water Initiative; Jael Silliman, author, scholar, and women's right activist; and Kissy Agyeman-Togobo, partner and cofounder of Songhai Advisory.

We are so grateful to our amazing agents Rafe Sagalyn and Jennifer Joel of ICM and Mel Berger of WME; our editors Niki Papadopoulos, Trish Daly, and Megan Mccormack of Penguin Random House; and our attorney, Neal Tabachnick, for going above and beyond to make sure this book made it into the hands of readers. Gina Zanolli and Rosemary Gudelj believed in this project and kept the forward momentum. They rallied support to bring it to life, alongside Kokovi Lawson, Heather Arney, Jennifer Schorsch, Vedika Bhandarkar, Rich Thorsten, Katrina Green, Zehra Shabbir, Lina Bonova, Melanie Mendrys, Andy Sareyan, and Paul O'Connell.

So many people lent their time and talent to this work along the way. Marla Smith-Nilson partnered with me to transform some one-off fundraising dinners into a real organization that grew into what is now Water.org. Volunteer staff joined very early on, including Dave Sarr, Brad Lessler, Julie Daniels, and Tracy Jackson. Jan and Susan Creidenberg ensured Water.org had office space when we first moved to Kansas City. Rania Anderson teamed with Jennifer Schorsch, Chevenee Reavis, Alix Lebec, and me to blend (and re-blend) our talents to powerful ends.

None of the far-reaching impact Water.org and WaterEquity have made would have been possible without the dedication and hard work of current and former staff members, board members, volunteers, contractors, and program partners throughout Africa, Southeast Asia, and Latin America. I wish we could name each one of you, for you were and are an indispensable part of the whole.

Thank you to the good people in the Department of Drinking Water and Sanitation, Ministry of Jal Shakti, India. Thank you to Bono and William Jefferson Clinton for challenging us to continue reaching for greater impact.

Thank you to the implementing partners who helped turn an unproven idea into actual programs changing millions of lives:

BASIX

CreditAccess Grameen

Equity Bank

ASA Philippines

MiBanco Peru

BURO Bangladesh

AMK Cambodia

DHAN India

PERPAMSI Indonesia

IDF India

Thank you to the strategic partners who fund our work:

PepsiCo Foundation

Caterpillar Foundation

IKEA Foundation

Inditex

InBev/Stella

Bank of America

Conrad N. Hilton Foundation

Skoll Foundation

MasterCard Foundation

Cartier Philanthropy

Niagara Bottling

#startsmall Foundation

Reckitt

Tarbaca Indigo Foundation

And finally, thank you to all who donate their hard-earned money to Water.org, whether it's $5 or $5,000,000. We hope this book has shown that you're investing in a better, more equal, more just planet for us all. And we are so grateful.

—GW

What Gary said.

I say that so often I should get a tattoo of it—but here, especially, I mean it from the bottom of my heart.

One of the most inspiring parts of doing this work has been seeing so many different people, from so many different backgrounds, imagine together how the world could be better, and then channel their own particular talents and energy and resources into making that vision a reality. I've seen firsthand how your work is changing lives. Thank you.

I am also deeply grateful to my wife, Lucy, and my daughters for their love and understanding. Thank you for sharing this life with me. I want to thank my brother, Kyle, and his wife, Lori, for their endless support and inspiration.

I owe so much to my mom, Nancy Carlsson-Paige, for setting me on a path of activism. It was her example that showed me I am here to do more than merely exist. And to my dad, Kent Damon—I wish he were here to let me know what he thinks of this book, and for a million other reasons.

—MD

Notes

Chapter One: What the Hell Is the "Water Issue"?

1. "Why a 'Water for Life' Decade?" United Nations Department of Economic and Social Affairs, 2005, https://www.un.org/waterforlifedecade/background.shtml.

2. Vickey Hallett, "Millions of Women Take a Long Walk with a 40-Pound Water Can," *Goats and Soda* (blog), NPR, July 7, 2016, https://www.npr.org/sections/goatsandsoda/2016/07/07/484793736/millions-of-women-take-a-long-walk-with-a-40-pound-water-can.

3. Mallika Kapur, "Some Indian Men Are Marrying Multiple Wives to Help Beat Drought," CNN, July 16, 2015, https://www.cnn.com/2015/07/16/asia/india-water-wives/index.html.

4. Patrick J. McDonnell, "Guatemala's Civil War Devastated the Country's Indigenous Maya Communities," *Los Angeles Times*, September 3, 2018, https://www.latimes.com/world/mexico-americas/la-fg-guatemala-war-aftermath-20180903-story.html.

5. Daniel B. Wroblewski, "One Year of Sanctuary in Cambridge, Mass.," *The Harvard Crimson*, April 11, 1986, https://www.thecrimson.com /article/1986/4/11/one-year-of-sanctuary-in-cambridge.

6. Li Liu, Hope L. Johnson, Simon Cousens, Jamie Perin, Susana Scott, Joy E. Lawn, Igor Rudan, Harry Campbell, Richard Cibulskis, Mengying Li, Colin Mathers, Robert E. Black, "Global, Regional, and National Causes of Child Mortality: An Updated Systematic Analysis for 2010 with Time Trends Since 2000," *The Lancet* 379, no. 9832 (2012), https://doi.org/10.1016/S0140-6736(12)60560-1.

7. Claire Chase and Richard Damania, "Water, Well-Being, and the Prosperity of Future Generations," World Bank Group, 2017, http://docu ments1.worldbank.org/curated/en/722881488541996303/pdf/WP -P155196-v1-PUBLIC-main.pdf.

8. Åsa Regnér, "We Must Leverage Women's Voice and Influence in Water Governance," UN Women, August 27, 2018, https://www.unwomen.org /en/news/stories/2018/8/speed-ded-regner-stockholm-world-water-week.

9. *The Human Development Report 2006* (New York: United Nations Development Programme, 2006), 22, http://hdr.undp.org/sites/default/files /reports/267/hdr06-complete.pdf.

10. Guy Hutton, "Global Costs and Benefits of Drinking-Water Supply and Sanitation Interventions to Reach the MDG Target and Universal Coverage" (Geneva: World Health Organization, 2012), 5, https://apps .who.int/iris/bitstream/handle/10665/75140/WHO_HSE_WSH _12.01_eng.pdf?sequence=1&isAllowed=y.

11. Anthony Kenny, *Ancient Philosophy: A New History of Western Philosophy, Volume I* (Oxford: Oxford University Press, 2007), 4.

12. David Foster Wallace, "2005 Kenyon Commencement Address" (speech, Kenyon College, Gambier, Ohio, May 21, 2005), https://web.ics.purdue .edu/~drkelly/DFWKenyonAddress2005.pdf.

13. Pauline Arrillaga, "Mercy or Murder? Doubts About a Death in Desert," *Los Angeles Times,* October 3, 1999, https://www.latimes.com/archives /la-xpm-1999-oct-03-mn-18196-story.html.

14. "Water," *Lapham's Quarterly* XI, no. 3 (2018): 14.

15. "3 Endure 4,000-Mile Run Across Sahara," CBS News, February 20, 2007, https://www.cbsnews.com/news/3-endure-4000-mile-run-across-sahara/.

16. *Running the Sahara*, directed by James Moll (New York: Gaia, 2007).

17. "Out of the Mouths of Babes: 'Aman Iman'—Water Is Life," *Running the Sahara*, December 12, 2006, http://www.runningthesahara.com/news .html#blog061212.

18. "Out of the Mouths of Babes," *Running the Sahara.*

19. "Water Resources Sector Strategy," The World Bank, last modified 2009, http://web.worldbank.org/archive/website01062/WEB/0__CO-47 .HTM?contentMDK=20729817&contTypePK=217265&folderPK =34004326&sitePK=494186&callCR=true%27.

Chapter Two: The Water Decade

1. Luke Dittrich, "Matt Damon: The Celebrity Shall Save You," *Esquire*, September 15, 2009, https://www.esquire.com/news-politics/a6286/matt -damon-1009/.

2. *Drinking-Water and Sanitation, 1981–1990: A Way to Health* (Geneva: World Health Organization, 1981), 2, https://apps.who.int/iris/bitstream /handle/10665/40127/9241560681_eng.pdf?sequence=1&isAllowed=y.

3. "New Decade Launched Seeks Clean Water, Proper Sanitation for All by 1990," *UN Monthly Chronicle* 18, no. 1 (January 1981): 29, https:// heinonline-org.stanford.idm.oclc.org/HOL/Page?collection=unl&handle =hein.unl/unchron0018&id=3&men_tab=srchresults.

4. Kenan Malik, "As a System, Foreign Aid Is a Fraud and Does Nothing for Inequality," *The Guardian*, September 2, 2018, https://www .theguardian.com/commentisfree/2018/sep/02/as-a-system-foreign -aid-is-a-fraud-and-does-nothing-for-inequality; https://www.washing tonpost.com/archive/politics/2001/01/26/aid-abroadis-businessback -home/e37a1548-fff2-4b00-861a-aab48ea0e5e5/.

5. Michael Dobbs, "Aid Abroad Is Business Back Home," *The Washington Post*, January 26, 2021, https://www.washingtonpost.com/archive/poli

tics/2001/01/26/aid-abroadis-businessback-home/e37a1548-fff2-4b00
-861a-aab48ea0e5e5.

6. UNDP Water Governance Facility, Stockholm International Water In-
stitute, "Accountability in WASH: Explaining the Concept," UNICEF,
September 2014, https://www.unicef.org/media/91311/file/Accountability
-in-WASH-Explaining-the-Concept.pdf.

7. John M. Kalbermatten, "The Water Decade," *Waterlines* 9, no. 3 (January 1991), https://www.ircwash.org/sites/default/files/Kalbermatten
-1991-Water.pdf.

8. *Achievements of the International Drinking Water Sanitation Decade
1981: Report of the Economic and Social Council: Report of the Secretary-
General* (New York: United Nations, 1990), 5, https://www.zaragoza.es
/contenidos/medioambiente/onu/1004-eng.pdf.

9. UNDP Water Governance Facility, "Accountability in WASH."

10. Guy Hutton and Mili Varughese, "The Costs of Meeting the 2030 Sustainable Development Goal Targets on Drinking Water Sanitation, and
Hygiene," Water and Sanitation Program technical paper (Washington,
DC: World Bank Group, 2016), 7, https://openknowledge.worldbank.org
/bitstream/handle/10986/23681/K8632.pdf?sequence=4&isAllowed=y.

11. *Financing Water and Sanitation in Developing Countries*, OECD, 2016,
https://www.oecd.org/dac/financing-sustainable-development/develop
ment-finance-topics/Financing%20water%20and%20sanitation
%20in%20developing%20countries%20-%20key%20trends%20and
%20figures.pdf.

12. David Bornstein, "The Real Future of Clean Water," *The New York
Times*, August 21, 2013, https://opinionator.blogs.nytimes.com/2013/08
/21/the-real-future-of-clean-water/.

Chapter Three: The Big Idea

1. Belinda Goldsmith and Meka Beresford, "War-Torn Afghanistan and
Syria Ranked Second and Third in the Thomson Reuters Foundation

Survey of About 550 Experts on Women's Issues," *Thomson Reuters Foundation News*, June 26, 2018, https://news.trust.org//item/20180612134519 -cxz54.

2. Apoorva Jadhav, Abigail Weitzman, and Emily Smith-Greenaway, "Household Sanitation Facilities and Women's Risk of Non-Partner Sexual Violence in India," *BMC Public Health* 16, no. 1139 (2016), https://bmcpublichealth.biomedcentral.com/articles/10.1186/s12889 -016-3797-z.

3. Peter Schwartzstein, "The Merchants of Thirst," *The New York Times*, January 11, 2020, https://www.nytimes.com/2020/01/11/business/drought -increasing-worldwide.html.

4. Schwartzstein, "The Merchants of Thirst."

5. Muhammad Yunus and Alan Jolis, *Banker to the Poor: Micro-Lending and the Battle Against World Poverty* (New York: Public Affairs, 2008).

6. Beth Duff-Brown, "Microcredit Bank Grows Out of a $27 Investment," *Los Angeles Times*, April 4, 2004, https://www.latimes.com/archives/la -xpm-2004-apr-04-adfg-banker4-story.html.

7. Yunus and Jolis, *Banker to the Poor.*

8. Muhammad Yunus, "Microcredit, Information Technology, and Poverty: The Experience of Grameen Bank," *The Brown Journal of World Affairs* 8, no 2 (2002), http://www.jstor.org/stable/24590258.

9. Rohini Pande and Erica Field, "Give Women Credit," *Ideas for India*, November 24, 2017, https://www.lse.ac.uk/about-lse/connect/assets/short hand-files/microfinance/index.html.

10. Yunus, "Microcredit, Information Technology, and Poverty."

11. David Lepeska, "The Maturation of Microfinance," *Devex*, July 16, 2008, https://www.devex.com/news/the-maturation-of-microfinance-29440.

12. Lepeska, "The Maturation of Microfinance."

13. Jason Burke, "Impoverished Indian Families Caught in Deadly Spiral of Microfinance Debt," *The Guardian*, January 31, 2011, https://www .theguardian.com/world/2011/jan/31/india-microfinance-debt -struggle-suicide.

14. "SKS Under Spotlight in Suicides," *The Wall Street Journal*, February 24, 2012, https://www.wsj.com/articles/SB1000142405297020391830457 7242602296683134.

15. Stephanie Wykstra, "Microcredit Was a Hugely Hyped Solution to Global Poverty. What Happened?," *Vox*, January 15, 2019, https://www.vox.com/future-perfect/2019/1/15/18182167/microcredit-microfinance-poverty-grameen-bank-yunus; Soutik Biswas, "India's Micro-Finance Suicide Epidemic," BBC, December 16, 2010, https://www.bbc.com/news/world-south-asia-11997571.

16. "Q&A with Muhammad Yunus," *Enterprising Ideas*, PBS, http://www.shoppbs.pbs.org/now/enterprisingideas/Muhammad-Yunus.html.

17. Don Johnston and Jonathan Morduch, "The Unbanked: Evidence from Indonesia," *The World Bank Economic Review* 22, no. 3 (2008): 520, http://www.jstor.org/stable/40282286.

18. Naren Karunakaran, "How to Fix Flaws in the Present Microfinance Model," *The Economic Times*, November 12, 2010, https://economictimes.indiatimes.com/industry/banking/finance/how-to-fix-flaws-in-the-present-microfinance-model/articleshow/6912025.cms?from=mdr.

19. "BASIX-Bhartiya Samruddhi Finance Limited (BSFL): A New Generation Livelihoods Promotion Institution," Growing Inclusive Markets, April 2010, http://www.growinginclusivemarkets.org/media/cases/India_BASIX_2011.pdf.

20. "The Cost of Leneriza's Water, Then and Now," Water.org, https://water.org/our-impact/all-stories/cost-lenerizas-water-then-and-now.

21. Meera Mehta, *Assessing Microfinance for Water and Sanitation: Exploring Opportunities for Sustainable Scaling Up* (Ahmedabad, India: Bill & Melinda Gates Foundation, 2008), 4, https://docs.gatesfoundation.org/documents/assessing-microfinance-wsh-2008.pdf.

Chapter Four: The Meet-Cute

1. Joe Conason, *Man of the World: The Further Endeavors of Bill Clinton* (New York: Simon & Schuster, 2016): 243–44.

2. "Press Release: President Clinton Announces Program for 2008 Clinton Global Initiative Annual Meeting," Clinton Foundation, September 15, 2008, https://www.clintonfoundation.org/main/news-and-media/press -releases-and-statements/press-release-president-clinton-announces -program-for-2008-clinton-global-initia.html.

3. "Parasitic Worms and Bono Jokes in Midtown Manhattan," *The Economist*, October 2, 2008, https://www.economist.com/news/2008/10/02 /billanthropy.

4. "Clinton Global Initiative Concludes with $8 Billion in Commitments," *Philanthropy News Digest*, September 30, 2008, https://philanthro pynewsdigest.org/news/clinton-global-initiative-concludes-with-8 -billion-in-commitments.

5. "Parasitic Worms and Bono Jokes," *The Economist*.

6. Sarah Haughn, "Clinton Global Initiative Commits Millions to Water and Sanitation," *Circle of Blue*, October 6, 2008, https://www.circleofblue .org/2008/world/clinton-global-initiative-commits-millions-to-water -and-sanitation.

7. "Delivering Access to Safe Water through Partnerships," Pepsico, 2014, https://www.pepsico.com/docs/album/sustainability-report/regional -and-topic-specific-reports/pep_wp14_safe_water_2014.pdf?sfvrsn =f59ded9f_4.

8. Guy Hutton and Mili Varughese, "The Costs of Meeting the 2030 Sustainable Development Goal Targets on Drinking, Water Sanitation, and Hygiene," Water and Sanitation Program technical paper (Washington, DC: World Bank Group, 2016), 2, https://openknowledge.worldbank.org /bitstream/handle/10986/23681/K8632.pdf?sequence=4&isAllowed=y.

9. *Financing Water and Sanitation in Developing Countries*, OECD, 2016, https://www.oecd.org/dac/financing-sustainable-development/develop ment-finance-topics/Financing%20water%20and%20sanitation %20in%20developing%20countries%20-%20key%20trends%20and %20figures.pdf.

10. Charles Fishman, *The Big Thirst* (New York: Free Press, 2012), 265.

11. Fishman, *The Big Thirst*, 266.

12. "How Much Water Is Needed in Emergencies," World Health Organization, last updated 2011, https://www.who.int/water_sanitation_health /publications/2011/tn9_how_much_water_en.pdf, https://handbook. spherestandards.org/en/sphere/#ch001.

13. Ken Bensinger, "Masses Aren't Buying Bailout," *Los Angeles Times*, September 16, 2008, https://www.latimes.com/archives/la-xpm-2008-sep -26-fi-voxpop26-story.html; Ben Rooney, "Bailout Foes Hold Day of Protests," CNN Money, September 25, 2008, https://money.cnn.com/2008 /09/25/news/economy/bailout_protests/?postversion=2008092517.

14. "Billanthropy Squared," *The Economist*, September 25, 2008, https:// www.economist.com/united-states/2008/09/25/billanthropy-squared.

15. Reuters Staff, "'Banker to Poor' Has Suggestion for Bankers to Rich," Reuters, September 26, 2008, https://www.reuters.com/article/us-financial -microfinance/banker-to-poor-has-suggestion-for-bankers-to-rich -idUSTRE48P7UK20080926.

Chapter Five: Water.org Begins

1. Brent Schrotenboer, "Livestrong Caught in Crossfire of Scandal, Says VP," *USA Today*, February 28, 2013, https://www.usatoday.com/story /sports/cycling/2013/02/28/lance-armstrong-livestrong-cancer-tour -de-france/1954665.

2. "Livestrong Charity Looks to Rebuild Following Lance Armstrong Scandal," Associated Press, February 11, 2020, https://www.espn.com /olympics/cycling/story/_/id/28680574/livestrong-charity-looks-rebuild -following-lance-armstrong-scandal.

3. "Household Water Use: Haiti," JMP, last updated 2020, https://wash data.org/data/household#!/table?geo0=country&geo1=HTI.

4. Richard Knox, "Water in the Time of Cholera: Haiti's Most Urgent Health Problem," NPR, April 12, 2021, https://www.npr.org/sections /health-shots/2012/04/13/150302830/water-in-the-time-of-cholera -haitis-most-urgent-health-problem.

5. Hans Rosling, *Factfulness: Ten Reasons We're Wrong About the World—and Why Things Are Better Than You Think* (New York: Flatiron Books, 2018), 15.

6. Rosling, *Factfulness*, 5–6.

7. Rosling, *Factfulness*, 9.

8. Max Roser (@MaxCRoser), "Newspapers could have had the headline 'Number of people in extreme poverty fell by 137,000 since yesterday' every day in the last 25 years," Tweet, October 16, 2017, https://twitter.com/MaxCRoser/status/919921745464905728.

Chapter Six: The Big Idea, Take Two

1. Kelly Dilworth, "Average Credit Card Interest Rates: Week of Aug. 4, 2021," CreditCards.com, August 4, 2021, https://www.creditcards.com/credit-card-news/rate-report.php.

2. "COVID-19 Spending Helped to Lift Foreign Aid to an All-Time High in 2020," OECD, April 13 2021, https://www.oecd.org/dac/financing-sustainable-development/development-finance-data/ODA-2020-detailed-summary.pdf.

3. "Despite COVID-19, Global Financial Wealth Soared to Record High of $250 Trillion in 2020," Boston Consulting Group, June 10, 2021, https://www.bcg.com/press/10june2021-despite-covid-19-global-financial-wealth-soared-record-high-250-trillion-2020.

4. Dan Ariely, *Predictably Irrational* (New York: Harper, 2009), 76.

5. Ariely, *Predictably Irrational*, 76.

6. Ariely, *Predictably Irrational*, 79.

7. Ariely, *Predictably Irrational*, 79.

8. OECD, "COVID-19 Spending Helped to Lift Foreign Aid to an All-Time High in 2020"; Boston Consulting Group, "Despite COVID-19, Global Financial Wealth Soared to Record High of $250 Trillion in 2020."

9. Steve Schueth, "Socially Responsible Investing in the United States," *Journal of Business Ethics* 43, no. 3 (2003): 189–94, http://www.jstor.org/stable/25074988; William Donovan, "The Origins of Socially

Responsible Investing," *The Balance*, April 23, 2020, https://www.the balance.com/a-short-history-of-socially-responsible-investing -3025578.https://www.jstor.org/stable/25074988.

10. Schueth, "Socially Responsible Investing," 189–94.

11. Donovan, "The Origins of Socially Responsible Investing."

12. Lena Williams, "Pressure Rises on Colleges to Withdraw South Africa Interests," *The New York Times*, February 2, 1986, https://www.nytimes .com/1986/02/02/us/pressure-rises-on-colleges-to-withdraw-south -africa-interests.html.

13. Paul Lansing, "The Divestment of United States Companies in South Africa and Apartheid," *Nebraska Law Review* 60, no. 2 (1981): 312, https:// digitalcommons.unl.edu/cgi/viewcontent.cgi?article=2025&context=nlr.

14. United States Congress, House Committee on Foreign Affairs, Subcommittee on International Economic Policy and Trade, "The Status of United States Sanctions Against South Africa: Hearing Before the Subcommittees on International Economic Policy and Trade and on Africa of the Committee on Foreign Affairs, House of Representatives, One Hundred Second Congress, First Session, April 30, 1991, Volume 4" (US Government Printing Office, 1992), https://books.google.com/books?id =itTyqdwa8CsC&pg=PA98&lpg=PA98&dq=south+africa+divestment +campaign+%2220+billion%22&source=bl&ots=kKgQRU9pIQ&sig =ACfU3U0NLoqA15ad2xuojwtd0WeM6wx0TA&hl=en&sa=X&ved =2ahUKEwizzY-I96HyAhWgElkFHaKmAooQ6AF6BAgMEAM#v =onepage&q=south%20africa%20divestment%20campaign%20 %2220%20billion%22&f=false.

15. Michiel A. Keyzer and C. Wesenbeeck, "The Millennium Development Goals, How Realistic Are They?" *De Economist* 165, no. 3 (February 2007), https://www.researchgate.net/publication/24110281_The _Millennium_Development_Goals_How_Realistic_Are_They.

16. *The Rockefeller Foundation 2005 Annual Report* (New York: Rockefeller Foundation, April 2006), https://www.rockefellerfoundation.org/wp -content/uploads/Annual-Report-2005-1.pdf.

17. *2005 Annual Report* (Bill & Melinda Gates Foundation, 2006), 38, https://www.gatesfoundation.org/-/media/1annual-reports/2005gates-foundation-annual-report.pdf.

18. Judith Rodin, *The Power of Impact Investing: Putting Markets to Work for Profit and Global Good* (Philadelphia: Wharton School Press, 2014); Veronica Vecchi, Luciano Balbo, Manuela Brusoni, and Stefano Caselli, eds., *Principles and Practice of Impact Investing: A Catalytic Revolution* (Sheffield, UK: Greenleaf Publishing, 2016).

19. "Bellagio Center," The Rockefeller Foundation: A Digital History, https://rockfound.rockarch.org/bellagio-center. https://www.rockefellerfoundation.org/our-work/bellagio-center/about-bellagio.

20. Beth Richardson, "Sparking Impact Investing Through GIIRS," *Stanford Social Innovation Review*, October 24, 2012, https://ssir.org/articles/entry/sparking_impact_investing_through_giirs.

21. "Thematic and Impact Investing Executive Summary," Principles for Responsible Development, https://www.unpri.org/thematic-and-impact-investing/impact-investing-market-map/3537.article.

22. Dan Freed, "JP Morgan's Dimon Rolls Eyes Up at Gloom and Davos Billionaires," Reuters, February 23, 2016, https://www.reuters.com/article/jpmorgan-outlook-davos/jp-morgans-dimon-rolls-eyes-up-at-gloom-and-davos-billionaires-idUSL8N16258B.

Chapter Seven: The World Moves

1. Richard Fry, "Millennials Are the Largest Generation in the U.S. Labor Force," Pew Research Center, April 11, 2018, https://www.pewresearch.org/fact-tank/2018/04/11/millennials-largest-generation-us-labor-force.

2. "3.1 Harnessing the Hype," in *From the Margins to the Mainstream: Assessment of the Impact Investment Sector and Opportunities to Engage Mainstream Investors* (Geneva: World Economic Forum, September 2013), 10, http://www3.weforum.org/docs/WEF_II_FromMargins Mainstream_Report_2013.pdf.

3. Abhilash Mudaliar and Hannah Dithrich, "Sizing the Impact Investing Market," Global Impact Investing Network, April 1, 2019, https://thegiin.org/research/publication/impinv-market-size.

4. World Economic Forum, "From the Margins to the Mainstream: Assessment of the Impact Investment Sector and Opportunities to Engage Mainstream Investors"; Mudaliar and Dithrich, "Sizing the Impact Investing Market"; Gary Shub, Brent Beardsley, Hélène Donnadieu, Kai Kramer, Monish Kumar, Andy Maguire, Philippe Morel, and Tjun Tang, "Global Asset Management 2013: Capitalizing on the Recovery," The Boston Consulting Group, July 2013, https://image-src.bcg.com/Images/Capitalizing_on_the_Recovery_Jul_2013_tcm9-95253.pdf; Renaud Fages, Lubasha Heredia, Joe Carrubba, Ofir Eyal, Dean Frankle, Edoardo Palmisani, Neil Pardasani, Thomas Schulte, Ben Sheridan, and Qin Xu, "Global Asset Management 2019: Will These '20s Roar?," July 2019, https://image-src.bcg.com/Images/BCG-Global-Asset-Management-2019-Will-These-20s-Roar-July-2019-R_tcm9-227414.pdf.

5. Somini Sengupta and Weiyi Cai, "A Quarter of Humanity Faces Looming Water Crisis," The New York Times, August 6, 2019, https://www.nytimes.com/interactive/2019/08/06/climate/world-water-stress.html?fallback=0&recId=1P6rWfI5kuGl6PAF5eQETnq2ONM&locked=0&geoContinent=NA&geoRegion=TX&recAlloc=top_conversion&geoCountry=US&blockId=most-popular&imp_id=64322975&action=click&module=trending&pgtype=Article&region=Footer.

6. Fiona Harvey, "Water Shortages to Be Key Environmental Challenge of the Century, Nasa Warns," The Guardian, May 16, 2018, https://www.theguardian.com/environment/2018/may/16/water-shortages-to-be-key-environmental-challenge-of-the-century-nasa-warns.

7. "AQUASTAT—FAO's Global Information System on Water and Agriculture," Food and Agriculture Organization of the United Nations, http://www.fao.org/aquastat/en/overview/methodology/water-use.

8. "AQUASTAT."

9. Sumila Gulyani, Debabrata Talukdar, and R. Mukami Kariuki, *Water for the Urban Poor: Water Markets, Household Demand, and Service Preferences in Kenya* (Washington, DC: The World Bank, 2005).

10. Richard Damania, Sébastien Desbureaux, Marie Hyland, Asif Islam, Scott Moore, Aude-Sophie Rodella, Jason Russ, and Esha Zaveri, *Uncharted Waters: The New Economics of Water Scarcity and Economic Variability* (Washington, DC: The World Bank, 2017), 36.

11. Henry Fountain, "Researchers Link Syrian Conflict to a Drought Made Worse by Climate Change," *The New York Times*, March 2, 2015, https://www.nytimes.com/2015/03/03/science/earth/study-links-syria -conflict-to-drought-caused-by-climate-change.html.

12. "How Could a Drought Spark a Civil War?," NPR, September 8, 2013, https://www.npr.org/2013/09/08/220438728/how-could-a-drought -spark-a-civil-war.

13. Joshua Hammer, "Is a Lack of Water to Blame for the Conflict in Syria?," *Smithsonian Magazine*, June 2013, https://www.smithsonianmag.com /innovation/is-a-lack-of-water-to-blame-for-the-conflict-in-syria -72513729.

14. Alexandra A. Taylor, "Climate Change Will Affect Access to Fresh Water. How Will We Cope?," *C&EN*, February 10, 2020, https://cen.acs .org/environment/water/Climate-change-affect-access-fresh/98/i6.

15. Carl Ganter, "Water Crises Are a Top Global Risk," World Economic Forum, January 16, 2015, https://www.weforum.org/agenda/2015/01/why -world-water-crises-are-a-top-global-risk/.

16. "High and Dry: Climate Change, Water, and the Economy," The World Bank, https://www.worldbank.org/en/topic/water/publication/high-and -dry-climate-change-water-and-the-economy.

17. "About," Water Resistance Coalition, https://ceowatermandate.org /resilience/about.

18. Ben Paynter, "Roughly One-Third of Funders Are Comfortable Taking Below-Market Rate Returns or Break-Even Paybacks," *Fast Company*, June 5, 2017, https://www.fastcompany.com/40426561/the-philanthropy

-world-is-embracing-impact-investing; Lori Kozlowski, "Impact Investing: The Power of Two Bottom Lines," *Forbes*, October 2, 2012, https://www.forbes.com/sites/lorikozlowski/2012/10/02/impact-investing-the-power-of-two-bottom-lines/?sh=7a4f037a1edc.

19. *The Sustainability Imperative* (New York: The Nielsen Company, 2015), 2, https://www.nielsen.com/wp-content/uploads/sites/3/2019/04/Global20 Sustainability20Report_October202015.pdf.

Chapter Eight: Venture Philanthropy

1. Nilanjana Bhowmick, "Handwashing Helps Stop COVID-19. But in India, Water Is Scarce," *National Geographic*, April 7, 2020, https://www.nationalgeographic.com/science/2020/04/hand-washing-can-combat-coronavirus-but-can-the-rural-poor-afford-frequent-rinses/.

2. "Almost 2 Billion People Depend on Health Care Facilities Without Basic Water Services," World Health Organization, December 14, 2020, https://www.who.int/news/item/14-12-2020-almost-2-billion-people-depend-on-health-care-facilities-without-basic-water-services-who-unicef.

3. Peter Daszak, "We Knew Disease X Was Coming. It's Here Now," *The New York Times*, February 27, 2020, https://www.nytimes.com/2020/02/27/opinion/coronavirus-pandemics.html.

4. Michael Dulaney, "The Next Pandemic Is Coming—and Sooner Than We Think, Thanks to Changes to the Environment," ABC News Australia, June 6, 2020, https://www.abc.net.au/news/science/2020-06-07/a-matter-of-when-not-if-the-next-pandemic-is-around-the-corner/12313372.

5. "Matt Struggles for Survival," *The Philippine Star*, September 5, 2011, https://www.philstar.com/entertainment/2011/09/05/723632/matt-struggles-survival.

6. Yagazie Emezi and Danielle Paquette, "Living Through a Pandemic When Your Access to Water Is Difficult," *The Washington Post*, May 21, 2020, https://www.washingtonpost.com/graphics/2020/world/nigeria-water-during-coronavirus/?itid=lk_interstitial_manual_71.

7. George McGraw, "How Do You Fight the Coronavirus Without Running Water?," *The New York Times*, May 2, 2020, https://www.nytimes .com/2020/05/02/opinion/coronavirus-water.html.

8. "The Challenge," United Nations Economic Commission for Europe, https://unece.org/challenge#:~:text=Methane%20is%20a%20power ful%20greenhouses,are%20due%20to%20human%20activities.

9. *Climate Change 2014: Mitigation of Climate Change* (New York: Cambridge University Press, 2014), https://www.ipcc.ch/site/assets/uploads /2018/02/ipcc_wg3_ar5_full.pdf.

10. "Greenhouse Gas Emissions from a Typical Passenger Vehicle," United States Environmental Protection Agency, July 21, 2021, https://www.epa.gov/greenvehicles/greenhouse-gas-emissions-typical -passenger-vehicle#:~:text=typical%20passenger%20vehicle%3F-,A %20typical%20passenger%20vehicle%20emits%20about%204.6 %20metric%20tons%20of,around%2011%2C500%20miles%20per %20year.

11. Mads Warming, "How Can More Water Treatment Cut CO2 Emissions?," International Water Association, May 20, 2020, https://iwa-network.org /how-can-more-water-treatment-cut-co2-emissions.

12. Sustainability at Manila Water: Protecting the Environment," Water Manila Company, 2019, https://reports.manilawater.com/2018/sustain ability-at-manila-water/protecting-the-environment.

13. "How Much Electricity Does an American Home Use?," U.S. Energy Information Administration, October 9, 2020, https://www.eia.gov/tools /faqs/faq.php?id=97&t=3.

14. Bill Kingdom, Roland Liemberger, and Philippe Marin, "The Challenge of Reducing Non-Revenue Water (NRW) in Developing Countries. How the Private Sector Can Help: A Look at Performance-Based Service Contracting," *Water Supply and Sanitation Sector Board Discussion Paper Series*, no. 8 (December 2006), 52, https://openknowledge .worldbank.org/bitstream/handle/10986/17238/394050Reducing1e0wa ter0WSS81PUBLIC1.pdf?sequence=1&isAllowed=y.

15. Katrina Yu, "Why Did Bill Gates Give a Talk with a Jar of Human Poop by His Side?," NPR, November 9, 2018, https://www.npr.org/sections/goatsandsoda/2018/11/09/666150842/why-did-bill-gates-give-a-talk-with-a-jar-of-human-poop-by-his-side.

16. "Vast Energy Value in Human Waste," United Nations University, November 2, 2015, https://unu.edu/media-relations/releases/vast-energy-value-in-human-waste.html.

17. "UN World Water Development Report 2020: 'Water and Climate Change,'" United Nations Water, March 21, 2020, https://www.unwater.org/world-water-development-report-2020-water-and-climate-change/.

18. James Workman, "Why Understanding Resilience Is Key to Water Management," *The Source*, April 13, 2017, https://www.thesourcemagazine.org/understanding-resilience-key-water-management/.

19. OECD and netFWD, "Venture Philanthropy in Development Dynamics, Challenges and Lessons in the Search for Greater Impact," OECD Development Centre, 2014, https://www.oecd.org/site/netfwd/Full%20Study_Venture%20Philanthropy%20in%20Development.pdf.

20. "World's Billionaires Have More Wealth Than 4.6 Billion People," Oxfam, January 20, 2020, https://www.oxfam.org/en/press-releases/worlds-billionaires-have-more-wealth-46-billion-people.

Chapter Nine: The Wave

1. *Slum Almanac 2015–2016: Tracking Improvement in the Lives of Slum Dwellers* (Nairobi: UN Habitat, 2016), 8, https://unhabitat.org/sites/default/files/documents/2019-05/slum_almanac_2015-2016_psup.pdf.

2. Sarah Bean Apmann, "Tenement House Act of 1901," *Village Preservation,* April 11, 2016. https://www.villagepreservation.org/2016/04/11/tenement-house-act-of-1901.

3. Rose George, *The Big Necessity* (New York: Picador, 2014), 242.

Index

Index

water.org ®

Giving the life-changing gift of safe water is the way to end poverty, achieve global equality and make a bright future possible **for all.**

Safe water gives women and girls time to learn, to earn and to create. Access to safe water enhances the resiliency of people living in poverty to the effects of climate change. And, access to safe water improves health and helps families protect themselves from illness and disease.

Water.org is a global nonprofit organization working to bring safe water and sanitation to the world. Donate to Water.org to give people in need access to safe water and the health, hope and opportunity that flow from it.

Donate now at **water.org/worthofwater**

Scan code
with phone

↓